AN ILLUSTRATED GUIDE TO
MODERN
SUBMARINES

The undersea weapons that rule the oceans today

David Miller

An Arco Military Book

PRENTICE HALL PRESS · New York

A Salamander Book

Copyright ©1987 by Salamander Books Ltd.

All rights reserved

An Arco Military Book

Published in 1987 by Prentice Hall Press
A Division of Simon & Schuster, Inc.
Gulf + Western Building
One Gulf + Western Plaza
New York, NY 10023

PRENTICE HALL PRESS is a trademark
of Simon & Schuster, Inc.

Previously published by Arco
Publishing, Inc.
Originally published by Salamander
Books Ltd., London.
This book may not be sold outside the
United States and Canada.

Library of Congress Catalog Card
Number: 81-71862

ISBN 0-668-05495-6

10 9 8 7 6 5 4 3 2 1

First Prentice Hall Press Edition

Contents

Submarines are arranged in three groups—SSBN/SSB/ SSGN/SSG; SS—and are listed, with minor variations, in alphabetical order of country of origin.

Credits

Author: Lt.Col. D.M.O. Miller has contributed numerous articles to technical defence journals and is co-author of Salamander's "The Balance of Military Power". (The publishers wish to thank John Jordan for his assistance in the preparation of this book)

Editor: Richard O'Neill

Designer: Barry Savage

Line drawings: © Siegfried Breyer

Photographs: The publishers wish to thank Captain J.E. Moore, RN, Antony Preston and all the official international governmental archives, weapons and systems manufacturers and private collections who supplied photographs for this book.

Printed by: Henri Proost et Cie, Turnhout, Belgium.

Introduction

For the first fifty years of its existence the submarine was a vessel which fought primarily on the surface, retiring underwater to hide or when under actual attack. Sonar (Asdic) was an imprecise instrument and ASW weapons were fairly ineffective, but a major problem for the submariner arose from the considerable speed advantage held by the surface ships. During World War II, the development of ship- and aircraft-mounted radar forced submarines beneath the surface, but the schnorkel tube enabled them to recharge their batteries at periscope depth, although their mast heads were detectable both visually and by radar. World War II saw also the appearance of the specialized ASW (anti-submarine warfare) aircraft as a most dangerous foe for the submerged submarine.

Freedom from regular forays to the surface for life support and propulsion came with the nuclear-powered steam plant, giving an endurance effectively limited only by psychological and physiological factors. This at last produced a really potent and truly underwater weapon system, capable of world-wide deployment and able to operate, at fleet speeds, with surface task groups. It also enabled submarines to travel submerged at speeds at least equal to, and frequently exceeding, those of attacking surface vessels.

Until the 1960s, submarines' primary strategic role was against maritime logistic traffic. Thus, in two World Wars, Germany brought the UK to the brink of starvation; in World War II, the US Navy won a great underwater victory against the Japanese. This role still exists, but the evolution of the ballistic missile submarine has brought a further strategic role, that of striking directly at targets in the enemy's homeland.

Missile Carriers

The USSR, while developing SSBNs like those of other navies, has also paid great attention to specially-developed cruise missile submarines. These boats have an anti-ship role and are intended mainly to counter US Navy carrier groups. The Americans, however, have avoided the need for such a submarine type by developing missiles (Tomahawk, Harpoon) which can be launched from a standard 21in (533mm) torpedo tube, thus making virtually every submarine a cruise missile carrier.

Finally, the conventionally-powered (diesel-electric) sub-

Abbreviations

AGSS	Auxiliary submarine.
ASW	Anti-submarine warfare.
MIRV	Multiple, independently targeted, re-entry vehicles.
MRV	Multiple re-entry vehicles.
MSBS	Mer-Sol Ballistique Strategique (French designation for SLBM).
SLBM	Submarine launched ballistic missile.
SLCM	Submarine launched cruise missile.

marine continues to thrive: many hundred are operational with some 39 navies. Very few countries can afford the increasingly expensive nuclear-powered boats, and only the US and French navies have announced any intention of all-nuclear underwater fleets.

Although submerged submarines are difficult to locate, there is no such thing as an undetectable submarine. All underwater craft give both acoustic and non-acoustic indications of their presence. Many countries are conducting expensive research programmes with a view to making detection of their submarines more difficult. Here NATO possesses a definite advantage, since Soviet submarines are inherently noisier; thus, NATO should be able to detect and identify the enemy first. Early confrontations of a possible future conflict are secretly rehearsed every day. Soviet SSNs endeavour to track Western SSBNs; NATO surface groups practise ASW techniques against tracking Soviet SSNs and SS; and, as the incident of the Soviet Whiskey class submarine grounding off Sweden's Karlskrona naval base showed in November 1981, clandestine reconnaissance missions regularly take place.

Battle for 'Inner Space'

The modern submarine is difficult to find, to identify and to sink. It has a global capability; in its current role, the SSBN is the ultimate deterrent, for its missiles threaten the enemy's cities and population in a second strike role. The oceans of the world are now designated 'inner space', since they are so vast and unexplored, and they are also becoming of ever-greater economic importance. It could well be that the battle for control of this difficult and alien environment is only just beginning and that the real age of the submarine is in its infancy.

This book sets out all the principal types of submarine in service or projected in the world's navies but for reasons of space some very minor types have been omitted. Submarines are split into three groups: SSBN/SSB; SSGN/SSG; SS. Within each group they are listed according to alphabetical order of country of origin (with minor variations, apparent in the full list of Contents on pages 4-5). Text and picture sections are also devoted to SLBMs and SLCMs. Each section is introduced by a brief survey of the current situation in the major navies.

SNLE	Sousmarin Nucleaire Lanceur d'Engins (French designation for SSBN).
SS	Submarine, conventionally (diesel-electric) powered.
SSB	Ballistic missile submarine, conventionally powered.
SSBN	Ballistic missile submarine, nuclear powered.
SSG	Cruise missile submarine, conventionally powered.
SSGN	Cruise missile submarine, nuclear powered.
SSN	Attack submarine, nuclear powered.

Strategic Missile Submarines

During 1955 the USSR began to convert six Zulu class submarines to fire ballistic missiles, fitting two launch tubes in the fin for the SS-N-4 (Snark). In the early 1950s the US Navy, in collaboration with the US Army, began development of the Jupiter ICBM, to be fuelled by liquid oxygen and kerosene: three of these 60ft (18.3m) surface-launched missiles were to be carried in a 10,000-ton nuclear submarine. The advent of the Soviet Zulu class made a US ballistic missile submarine more urgently required, and, fortunately, developments in solid fuel and miniaturization led to the Polaris A-1 SLBM. Not only did this have solid fuel with all its attendant advantages, it could also be launched submerged and had a range of 1,380 miles (2,220km). Finally, it was so small that 16 could be carried in the hull of a submarine half the size of that required by the Jupiter missiles.

The submerged launch capability and the (for that period) long range of the Polaris A-1 meant that these submarines were virtually undetectable until they launched the missiles. SSBNs are still virtually undetectable They normally make fairly fast transits to their operational areas and then cruise at about 2 to 3 knots (3.75 to 5.6km/hr), adjusting their depth according to varying water conditions to make detection as difficult as possible. Their main problem is the maintenance of an incoming communications link to ensure that they can receive information and, in the final resort, orders to fire. In the US case, at least, this involves trailing a long wire antenna near the surface, which, of course, makes the SSBN more susceptible to detection. It can be assumed that SSNs will frequently operate in company with SSBNs, in order to protect them.

All SSBNs now launch their missiles from beneath the surface, firing one missile at a time in a sequential salvo. French SSBNs can fire all 16 SLBMs in 15 minutes; US Poseidon boats fire one every 50 seconds (total: 12 minutes 30 seconds).

All the Western SSBNs have two crews, alternately on patrol or on leave and retraining. This ensures maximum sea-time for the boats but, even so, about one-third of the force is always in port for maintenance, crew changeover or major refit. The USA currently maintains some 55 per cent of its SSBNs at sea, and this should increase to 65 per cent when sufficient Ohios join the fleet. The USSR maintains only about 13 to 15 SSBNs at sea. Obviously, in a period of tension both superpower navies would rush more boats to sea, an act which in itself would increase the international tension.

United States of America

There are 31 Lafayette class SSBNs in service. Constructed between 1961 and 1966 and mounting 16 Polaris A-2 SLBMs, the whole class was converted to take Poseidon C-3 between 1969 and 1978. The next stage is the further conversion of 12 boats to carry Trident C-4 missiles: the first of these (USS *Francis Scott Key*) rejoined the fleet as an operational Trident SSBN in October 1979 and the last of the group will rejoin by the end of 1982.

Purpose-built for the Trident missile, the Ohio class (18,700 tons submerged displacement) was thought to be large until the Soviet Typhoon class of 25,000 tons was revealed in 1981. USS *Ohio* commenced sea-trials in late 1981 and first fired Trident in mid-January 1982. Eight Ohios have so far been authorized. Each carries 24 Trident missiles and the hull design is much quieter than previous SSBNs, making acoustic detection much more difficult. The great increase in range (Trident: 3,831nm, 7,100km; Poseidon: 2,800nm, 5,200km) means that Trident submarines can

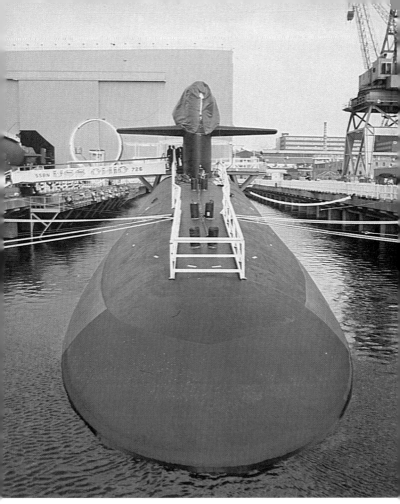

Above: USS *Ohio* (SSBN-726), the USN's first Trident missile submarine, awaits her naming ceremony, April 1979.

operate at much greater distances from the USSR, remaining in what amount to American-dominated waters. Research and development into future systems continues: one prospect under examination is a smaller, cheaper SSBN, but one that will be still capable of carrying 24 Trident missiles.

The US Navy's Polaris/Poseidon/Trident force has up to now given America reasonable assurance of a second-strike capability. There has been some concern over the survivability of the communications systems, but this problem has been overcome (it is hoped) by multiplicity of means and a high degree of redundancy. Navigation

and precise position-finding problems are slowly being mastered, to the extent that the USSR may well become concerned over the possibility of US SSBNs achieving the capability of a counterforce first-strike against hardened targets. This is reinforced by President Reagan's decision in late 1981 to authorize development and production of the Trident II (D-5) missile for deployment in 1989.

United Kingdom and France

The UK's Polaris force of four Resolution class SSBNs, each armed with 16 Polaris A-3, was commissioned between 1967 and

1969. The missiles themselves were purchased direct from the USA, but the warheads and re-entry vehicles are designed and manufactured in the UK, thus giving the British Government ultimate national control over deployment, launching and targeting, although normally the Polaris force is "assigned" to NATO. A fifth boat was cancelled in 1965.

The effectiveness of the UK strategic force is maintained by an interim programme which has upgraded the effectiveness of the re-entry vehicles and warheads. In the longer term the UK will purchase Trident missiles from the USA, but, as with Polaris, British warheads will be installed. These missiles will be deployed in new British SSBNs; four are currently planned and decision on a fifth will be made in 1982-83. Construction will begin in 1987, with an IOC in the early 1990s and a life expectancy through to 2020. The four-boat programme will cost some £5,000 million; a fifth boat would add another £600 million. However, the American decision to proceed with Trident II faces the UK with the possibility of a much more expensive programme; possibly as much as an extra £1,000 million at 1980 prices.

France's nuclear deterrent has been developed entirely within her own resources, a truly remarkable achievement. The first SSBN, *Le Redoutable*, became operational in 1971 and her first three sisters joined the fleet in 1973, 1974 and 1976. Unlike the British, the French then decided to build a fifth boat which became operational in May 1980. A sixth, *L' Inflexible*, a more advanced design, is now under construction and should be launched in mid-1982 and President Mitterand recently authorized construction of a seventh boat for delivery in 1986. The French then envisage an entirely new class which, like the British Trident boats, will enter service in the early 1990s and serve through until at least the 2020s.

Keeping sufficient SSBNs at sea is a problem for the US Navy with 36 boats; it is much more critical

Communicating with Submarines

One of the most critical aspects of SSBN operations is to seek to guarantee communications in a nuclear war; this diagram shows some of the complicated and expensive methods available to the USA. Highest authority is the National Command Authority, which is backed up by the National Emergency Airborne Command Post (A). Orders can then be passed through the National Military Command Centre or its Alternate. CINCPAC, CINCLANT and CINCSAC also have airborne command posts (B). The Defense Communications System (DCS) has ground-based transmitters operating in the High (C), Low (D), Very Low (E) and Extremely Low (F) Frequency bands. There are also communications through the Defense (G), Air Force (H), and Fleet (J) satellite systems. Relays are also possible through the TACAMO system (K), surface ships (L), or the Emergency Rocket Communications System (M). This complex system is the price to be paid for a viable and credible second-strike nuclear deterrent.

for the smaller British and French navies. The Royal Navy guarantees to have one boat on patrol at all times, frequently with a second also at sea; it could probably get a third to sea in time of crisis. The French, however, have publicly stated that they must have six hulls in order to ensure that three SSBNs are continuously available, of which two will be on patrol. In view of the minimal number of boats actually on patrol simultaneously, both navies would be very badly affected if the USSR should make a technological breakthrough in the ASW field.

Soviet Union

The first true ballistic missile submarines were the Soviet Navy's diesel-engined Golf class, of which only two now remain in the strategic role. Their first nuclear submarines were the Hotel class, of which seven Hotel II and one Hotel III survive. SLBMs in the Golf and Hotel class submarines all count towards the SALT missile limits, although the Golf class hulls do not count towards the launch platform totals specified.

The Yankee class appeared in 1968 and 34 were completed by 1976. Far more formidable than the Golf and Hotel classes, the

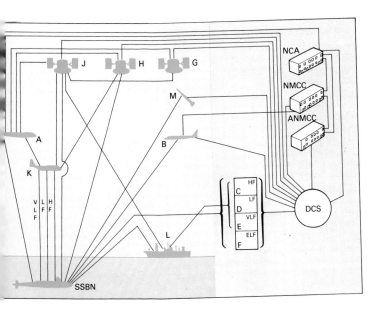

Yankees' shortcomings are their rather bulky missiles (SS-N-6), which lack range compared with Polaris. This means that Yankee I must deploy close to the US coast to obtain good coverage of targets such as SAC bases, although a coincidental advantage is a short missile flight (6 to 10 minutes) which effectively prevents counter-surprise scrambles at the bomber airfields. Yankee I SSBNs are, however, already being deactivated as new Delta IIIs join the fleet, to keep within SALT limits, and five have so far been converted to SSN configuration. One Yankee II is fitted with the experimental SS-NX-17.

The prototype of the Typhoon class was launched in September 1980; a monster of 25,000 tons submerged displacement, it is three times the size of Delta III and some 40 per cent larger than the US Navy's Ohio class. Typhoon is reported to carry 20 of a new type of missile *forward* of the fin and may herald a new Soviet strategic concept for SSBN/SLBM deployment.

Some 13 Soviet SSBN/SSB are normally on patrol: possible distribution may be three in the Pacific, five in the Barents Sea and five in the North Atlantic. Western navies mount a very sophisticated operation to find and track these SSBNs,

the task being facilitated by the generally poor design of the Soviet hulls which generate considerable noise, although improvements in this area are reported. The SS-N-18 missile has such a range that Delta III SSBNs can cover targets in CONUS from the Barents Sea and the Sea of Okhotsk, which provide them with much greater protection. The Barents Sea is currently an effective haven because of its proximity to the USSR, its distance from NATO bases and the generally inhospitable environment. Its shallowness inhibits the effectiveness of long-range ASW, while the sea ice covering large areas inhibits the deployment of sonobuoys and devices such as RDSS. The Sea of Okhotsk is not quite such a secure haven, but its use by SSBNs explains why the USSR so resolutely retains occupied Japanese territory in Sakhalin.

People's Republic of China

The only other navy with a potential for producing SSBN/SLBM is China, although there is no evidence to date of any such boats being constructed. Nevertheless, it seems an obvious step in China's progress towards super-power status, and within her capability.

Resolution Class

Total built:	Four.
Launched:	1966-80.
Status:	Four in service.
Displacement:	7,500 tons (surfaced); 8,400 tons (submerged).
Dimensions:	Length, 425ft (129.5m); beam, 33ft (10.1m); draught, 30ft (9.1m).
Missiles:	16 Polaris A-3.
Torpedo tubes:	Six 21in (533mm) bow.
Propulsion:	Nuclear (15,000shp).
Shafts:	One.
Speed:	20kt, 37km/hr (surfaced); 25kt, 46km/hr (submerged).
Complement:	143.

In the late 1950s it was planned that the RAF would provide the British strategic deterrent in the 1960s and 1970s, using V-bombers armed with the Skybolt missile. But at the Nassau Conference in 1962, President Kennedy told Britain that the USA was abandoning Skybolt because of apparently insuperable development problems. It was then agreed that Britain would build her own SSBNs: the USA was to provide Polaris SLBMs which would, however, have an entirely British front end.

Four submarines were built of a planned total of five, the last boat being cancelled in the Labour government's defence review in 1965. Much technical assistance was obtained from the USA and the Resolution class is generally similar to the American Lafayette class SSBNs, although the Resolutions' actual design is based on that of the Valiant SSN, but with a missile compartment between the control centre and the reactor room.

In the longer term the UK intends to purchase Trident missiles from the USA, but as with Polaris, an entirely British warhead will be installed. These missiles will be deployed in new British SSBNs; four are currently planned, but a decision on a fifth will be made in 1982-83. Construction of the SSBNs will begin in 1987 with an IOC in the early 1990s and a life expectancy through to 2020 at least.

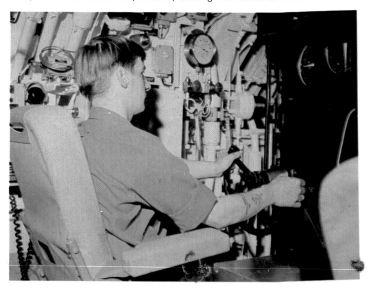

Above: HMS *Resolution*, the Royal Navy's first nuclear-powered ballistic missile submarine, commissioned on 2 October 1967.

Below left: RN rating at the controls of HMS *Repulse*, second of the four Resolution class SSBNs to enter serivce, in 1968.

Below: The Resolutions carry sixteen Polaris SLBMs; a new Trident-armed SSBN class will begin construction in 1987.

Le Redoutable Class

Total built:	Five.
Launched:	1967-77.
Status:	Five in service.
Displacement:	8,045 tons (surfaced); 8,940 tons (submerged).
Dimensions:	Length, 422ft 5in (128.7m); beam, 34ft 10in (10.6m); draught, 32ft 10in (10m).
Missiles:	Sixteen MSBS M-20.
Torpedo tubes:	Four 21.7in (550mm).
Propulsion:	Nuclear (16,000shp); reserve diesel (1,306shp).
Shafts:	One.
Speed:	25kt, 46km/hr (submerged).
Complement:	135.

Like Britain, France decided to build nuclear ballistic missile submarines to ensure a viable national nuclear deterrent; but unlike the British Polaris and Trident submarines, the French *'Force de dissuasion'* has been developed completely independently of the USA. This has resulted in a much greater effort spread over a much longer timescale, and in heavier missiles carrying a smaller warhead over a shorter range. The Mer-Sol Ballistique Strategique (MSBS) M-1 SLBM fitted in the first two boats had a range of only 1,500 miles (2,400km), but this has been progressively increased in successive missile systems. The first four boats were all modified to take the MSBS M-2, but have subsequently been modified again to take the M-20. The fifth boat was constructed from the outset to take the latter missile.

An even better missile—the M-4—with a MIRVed warhead was tested in the experimental diesel-electric submarine *Gymnote* in 1978-79. This submarine has been used to develop the Le Redoutable boats and their missiles. Built between 1963 and 1966, it has two SLBM launching tubes and a laboratory suite.

The Le Redoutable boats resemble the American SSBNs in that they have two rows of eight vertical SLBM launch tubes abaft the fin, which carries the forward hydroplanes. The French SSBNs have turbo-electric propulsion, but also have an auxiliary diesel that can be cut in to provide power should the nuclear reactor fail.

An order was placed in late 1978 for a sixth SSBN of a more advanced design and this boat, *L'Inflexible,* will enter service in 1985. Then, on 13 November 1981, following a two-day visit to *Le Tonnant* on an operational patrol, the French Prime Minister announced an order for a seventh SSBN, also of the interim class, for delivery in the mid-1980s—a clear endorsement by the Socialist government of France's independent nuclear deterrent. It is planned to replace all five first-generation boats with a totally new class in 1990-2000, with the sixth interim design being replaced later.

The French SSBN/SLBM programme is a major national achievement, although it is also one which has been achieved at a great price.

Below left: The diesel-electric test boat *Gymnote* prepares for trials with the MSBS M-4 SLBM, which is planned to be carried by all Redoutables except the name-boat from 1987 on.

Below right: *Le Redoutable.* The five SSBNs of this class will be joined by two improved L'Inflexible SSBNs in the mid-1980s.

Typhoon Class

Total built:	One (+?).
Launched:	1980 onward.
Status:	Fitting out.
Displacement:	25,000 tons (submerged).
Dimensions:	Length, 558ft (170m); beam, 75ft (22.9m); draught, not known.
Missiles:	Twenty SS-N-18 or twenty SS-NX-20.
Torpedo tubes:	Six or eight 21in (533mm).
Propulsion:	Nuclear (75,000shp, estimated).
Speed:	24kt, 44km/hr (submerged).
Complement:	150.

Persistent and growing rumours in the West were confirmed by the NATO announcement in November 1980 that the USSR had launched the first of the Typhoon class SSBNs. This enormous craft has a submerged displacement of 25,000 tons and an overall length of 558ft (170m), making it by far the largest submarine ever built. Among the many unusual features of the design is the 75ft (22.9m) beam; the normal length: beam ratio in SSBNs is in the region of 13:1, but the extraordinary girth of the Typhoon reduces the ratio to 7:1. This may indicate a considerable degree of separation (up to 14-15ft, 4.3-4.57m) between outer and inner hulls, or simply a huge inner hull.

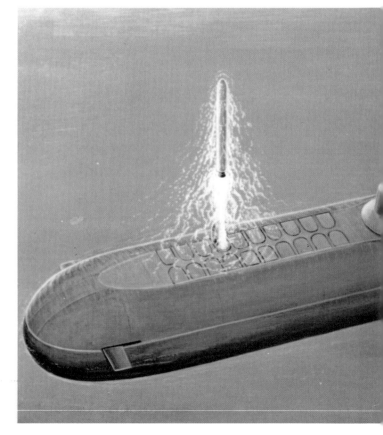

Another departure from previous practice is that the 20 missile tubes are forward of the fin. The reason for this is not yet clear, although one possibility is that the propulsion machinery for this giant is so large and heavy that the missile compartment has had to be moved forward to compensate.

If it were to venture out into the open oceans, this submarine would be relatively easy for NATO to follow: its very size would facilitate detection by virtually every type of ASW sensor. It seems possible, therefore, that it is simply intended as a relatively invulnerable missile launching platform, required only to move a short distance out into the Barents Sea and to loiter there, its time on station limited only by the endurance of the crew. For the latter, conditions can be assumed to be more spacious and comfortable than in any previous type of SSBN. And this, in fact, suggests another possibility: that the Typhoon might be designed to operate for a protracted period a long way from its bases. The 4,500-mile (7,240km) range of the SS-NX-20 SLBM would certainly enable the Typhoon to operate in the southern oceans, thus posing an entirely new threat to the USA.

It is worth noting that the Russians have frequently exhibited a fascination with sheer size and their latest ships—Kirov (battle-cruiser), Kiev (aircraft carrier), Oscar (SSGN)—seem to fit in with such a general pattern.

Below: Artist's impression of the 25,000-ton Typhoon class SSBN, with 20 forward-mounted tubes for SS-N-18 or SS-NX-20 SLBMs.

Delta Class

Total built:	Delta I: 18; Delta II: 4; Delta III: 11 (+1).
Launched:	Delta I: 1973-77; Delta II: 1973-75; Delta III: 1976-?
Status:	Delta I: 18 in service; Delta II: 4 in service; Delta III: 12 in service.
Displacement:	Delta I: 8,600 tons (surfaced), 10,000 tons (submerged); Delta II: 9,600 tons (surfaced), 11,400 tons (submerged); Delta III: 11,000 tons (surfaced), 13,250 tons (submerged).
Dimensions:	Delta I: length, 446ft 1in (136m); beam, 38ft (11.6m); draught, 32ft 10in (10m). Delta II: length, 500ft 11in (152.7m); beam, 38ft 8in (11.8m); draught, 33ft 6in (10.2m). Delta III: length, 509ft (155.1m); beam, 39ft 5in (12m); draught, 33ft 5in (10.2m).
Missiles:	Delta I: twelve SS-N-8; Delta II: sixteen SS-N-8; Delta III: sixteen SS-N-18.
Torpedo tubes:	Delta I/II/III: six 21in (533mm).
Propulsion:	Delta I/II/III: nuclear (60,000shp).
Shafts:	Delta I/II/III: two.
Speed:	Delta I/II: 25kt, 46km/hr (submerged); Delta III: 24kt, 44.5km/hr (submerged).
Complement:	Delta I: 120; Delta II/III: 132.

Until 1973 the US Navy had a considerable advantage in the quality and performance of its SLBMs, but in that year the Soviet Navy introduced the SS-N-8 missile with a range of more than 4,800 miles (7,720km) and a CEP of only 0.84nm (1,550m). This outranges not only Poseidon but Trident 1 as well. Initial trials were conducted in a Hotel III class SSBN and the missile system was then installed in the Delta I and Delta II class. The Delta I carries twelve missiles in two rows of six abaft the fin; the Delta II carries four more, matching the Western SSBNs with their sixteen missiles. A second slipway was built at the Severodvinsk shipyard in 1975 to enable these boats to be built more quickly.

The Delta III is somewhat larger than the Delta II and carries 16 SS-N-18 missiles which have a range of some 5,900 miles (9,500km) and mount MIRVed warheads. These submarines are a great threat to the USA because they can hit North America from launching areas in the Sea of Okhotsk and the Barents Sea, well out of reach of any known countermeasures.

Above right: The large casing abaft the fin of the Delta I ballistic missile submarine is necessary for the accommodation of two rows of six launch tubes for the SS-N-8 SLBM, which has an overall length of 42ft 6in (12.95m).

Centre: Determined to match the SLBM capacity of Western SSBNs, the Soviets introduced the Delta II in 1973. An increase of some 55ft (17m) in the length of the missile casing abaft the fin permitted the housing of sixteen SS-N-8 missiles.

Right: A little larger than Delta II, Delta III also has a higher missile casing to accommodate sixteen launch tubes for the 46ft 4in (14.1m) long SS-N-18 missile, with up to seven MIRVed warheads and a range of c5,900 miles (9,500km).

Yankee Class

Total built:	Yankee I (SSBN): 33; Yankee II (SSBN): 1; Yankee III (SSN): 5 (Yankee I conversions).
Launched:	Yankee I: 1966-71; Yankee II: 1975; Yankee III: converted 1978-81.
Status:	Yankee I: 28 in service; Yankee II: 1 in service; Yankee III: 5 in service.
Displacement:	Yankee I/II: 7,800 tons (surfaced), 9,300 tons (submerged); Yankee III: c4,600 tons (surfaced), c5,600 tons (submerged).
Dimensions:	Yankee I/II: length, 424ft 7in (129.4m); beam, 38ft (11.6m); draught, 25ft 7in (7.8m). Yankee III: length, 329ft 7in (100.5m); beam, 38ft (11.6m); draught, c25ft (7.6m).
Missiles:	Yankee I: sixteen SS-N-6; Yankee II: twelve SS-N-17; Yankee III: nil.
Torpedo tubes:	Yankee I/II/III: six 21in (533mm).
Propulsion:	Yankee I/II/III: nuclear (40,000shp).
Shafts:	Yankee I/II/III: two.
Speed:	Yankee I/II: 20kt, 37km/hr (surfaced), 30kt, 55.5km/hr (submerged); Yankee III: 20kt, 37km/hr (surfaced), 30+ kt, 55.5km/hr (submerged).
Complement:	Yankee I/II: 120; Yankee III: c90.

The Yankee class were the first Soviet purpose-designed nuclear ballistic missile submarines to enter service, and (a decade after the Americans) they were the first Soviet submarines to mount SLBMs within the hull. The sixteen missiles are arranged in two vertical rows of eight abaft the fin in a similar fashion to the US Polaris boats. The first twenty boats were armed with the SS-N-6 Mod I (Sawfly) SLBM which has one 1 to 2MT warhead and a range of some 1,495 miles (2,405km). The next thirteen boats mounted the longer-ranged SS-N-6 Mod 3 which has two MRV warheads, while the last of the class mounted twelve SS-N-17 in a trial installation.

Like all Soviet boats, the Yankees are noisier than their Western counterparts and are correspondingly easier to detect. The relatively short range of the SS-N-6, even in its later versions, means that the Yankees must approach the American coast before launching their missiles, although they are less vulnerable than the earlier boats which had to surface to launch their missiles.

Since 1978 five Yankees have had their missile section removed, thus shortening them by 95ft (28.9m), and they are now employed as SSNs. This conversion is intended to keep the Soviet strategic missile force within the SALT limits, especially in view of the impending entry into service of the Typhoon class, each carrying twenty missiles.

Top: Entering service from late 1967 onward, the Yankee class boats were the Soviet Navy's first purpose-designed nuclear ballistic submarines, able to fire their sixteen SS-N-6 Mod 1 (Sawfly) SLBMs while remaining submerged.

Above: The caps of the missile tubes can be seen abaft the fin of this Yankee. The Yankee I boats each carry sixteen SS-N-6 Mod 1 or Mod 3 SLBMs in two vertical rows of eight.

Left: The missile section abaft the fin, visible in its entirety in this picture, has been removed from the five Yankee III boats converted to SSNs in 1978-1981.

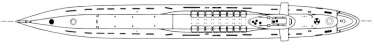

Yankee I class SSBN.

Hotel II/III Class

Total built:	Hotel II, 7; Hotel III, 1.
Launched:	1957-61.
Status:	Eight in service.
Displacement:	4,750 tons (surfaced); 5,600 tons (submerged).
Dimensions:	Length, 377ft 2in (115m); beam, 29ft 10in (9.1m); draught, 25ft (7.6m).
Missiles:	Hotel II, three SS-N-5; Hotel III, six SS-N-8.
Torpedo tubes:	Six 21in (533mm) bow; two 16in (406mm) stern.
Propulsion:	Nuclear (25,000shp).
Shafts:	Two.
Speed:	26kt, 48km/hr (submerged).
Complement:	90.

This class was completed in the years 1958-62 as the Hotel I, armed with SS-N-4 (Snark) missiles. These were mounted vertically in three tubes which were fitted between the keel and the top of the fin. The submarine had to surface to launch its missiles, which were blown out of the tube by explosive charges prior to main motor ignition.

Being clearly less than satisfactory as an SLBM system, the boats were converted in 1962-67 to Hotel II standard, to take the SS-N-5 (Serb) system, which is launched while submerged, with a range of some 994 miles (1,600km). The Hotel IIs were deployed off the Western and Eastern seaboards of North America, posing a threat to US strategic bomber bases, especially as missile flight times would have been some 6-10 minutes. So far as is known, the Hotel IIs have been withdrawn from these areas and are now assigned against 'theatre' targets in Western Europe and the Far East.

One Hotel II was converted to take six SS-N-8 missiles and was designated Hotel III. It was a test-bed for the missiles, which are now standard armament on Yankee and Delta I/II SSBNs. All Hotel II and III class submarines count towards SALT totals.

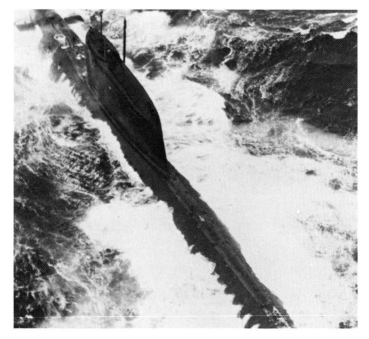

Above: Apparently surfaced because of damage, this Hotel II SSBN was seen some 600 miles NE of Newfoundland, February 1972.

Below left: Hotel II carries three fin-mounted SS-N-5 SLBMs.

Below: Hotel II under way. A single Hotel class converted as a test-bed for SS-N-8 missiles was designated Hotel III.

Hotel II SSBN.

Golf Class

Total built:	21 (+?).
Launched:	1959-63.
Status:	19 in service (three Golf I(Mod); thirteen Golf II; one Golf III; one Golf IV; one Golf V).
Displacement:	2,350 tons (surfaced); 2,850 tons (submerged).
Dimensions:	Length, 321ft 5in (98m); beam, 27ft 11in (8.5m); draught, 21ft (6.4m).
Missiles:	Golf I(Mod), none; Golf II, three SS-N-5; Golf III, three SS-N-8; Golf IV, three SS-N-6; Golf V, three S-NX-?.
Torpedo tubes:	Six 21in (533mm).
Propulsion:	Three diesel (6,000shp); three electric (12,000shp).
Shafts:	Three.
Speed:	17kt, 31.5km/hr (surfaced); 14kt, 26km/hr (submerged).
Complement:	87.

The Golf I conventionally powered submarines were built at the same time and with the same weapons system as the Hotel class, possibly as an insurance against the failure of the then new concept of nuclear propulsion. The short range of the SS-N-4 (426 miles, 685km) was always a marked disadvantage and, following completion of the conversion programme of Hotel I to Hotel II in 1967, 13 Golf class SSBs were also converted to take three SS-N-5. It was one of these boats that sank in the Pacific in 1968 and was later partially raised in a clandestine CIA operation in 1974. At least six Golf IIs are usually deployed in the Baltic with the balance in the Pacific, presumably all with a theatre role.

One Golf I was later modified to launch SS-N-8 (as Golf III); another to launch SS-N-6 (Golf IV); and a third to take a new type of missile, possibly the SS-NX-20 intended for the Typhoon class. The missiles in the Golf III and IV boats count towards the SLBM totals in the SALT I missile limits, but the Golf hulls themselves are not included in the launch platform aggregate.

Finally, at least one and probably all three of the remaining Golf Is have been modified by the removal of the missiles and the addition of numerous antennae, including one on a special mounting on the stern. In addition the rear of the fin has been cut away to form two steps. These boats are designated Golf I (Modified).

At least one Golf class SSB has been built in China, although whether it has been fitted with missiles has never been clarified. A Golf class submarine of the PLA-Navy exploded in the South China Sea in mid-1981, possibly in the course of missile tests.

Top: Close-up view of one of the 13 Golf class diesel-electric submarines converted by the Soviets to Golf II SSBs, with three SS-N-5 SLBM launch tubes mounted in the fin.

Above: The short range of the SS-N-4 SLBMs mounted in the Golf I SSB, seen here, soon led to further conversions of the class.

Left: Golf II SSN. Only the SS-N-8 and SS-N-6 missiles of Golf III and IV count towards SLBM totals agreed in SALT I.

Golf II SSN.

Ohio Class

Total built:	1 (3 building; 4 on order; 8 more projected).
Launched:	1979 onward.
Status:	One in service, three fitting out.
Displacement:	16,600 tons (surfaced); 18,700 tons (submerged).
Dimensions:	Length, 560ft (170.7m); beam, 42ft (12.8m); draught, 35ft 6in (10.8m).
Missiles:	24 Trident 1 (C-4).
Torpedo tubes:	Four 21in (533mm).
Propulsion:	Nuclear (60,000shp).
Shafts:	One.
Speed:	Not known.
Complement:	133.

While the programme of upgrading the later Polaris SLBM submarines to carry Poseidon was under way in the early 1970s, development of an entirely new missile was started. This was to have a much longer range—4,400 miles (7,100km)—which in turn necessitated a new and much larger submarine to carry it. The missile, Trident 1, is now in service on converted Lafayette class SSBNs, while the first of the submarines purpose-built for Trident, USS *Ohio,* has just joined the fleet. Initially Congress baulked at the immense cost of the new system—but then the Soviet Navy introduced its own long-range SLBM, the 4,200-mile (6,760km) SS-N-8, in the Delta class. This was followed in 1976 by the firing of the first of the increased-range SS-N18s (4,846 miles, 7,800km). US reaction was to speed up the Trident programme, and the first of the Ohio class submarines was laid down on 10 April 1976. One is now on trials—firing its first Trident at sea in mid-January 1982—three are fitting out, four have been laid down, and orders for eight more are likely.

Top: Port bow view of the monster USS *Ohio* (SSBN-726) while under construction at Groton, Connecticut, late in 1978.

Above: Precommissioning activity aboard *Ohio,* October 1981. In the control room, three crewmen simulate diving operations. This SSBN has a diving depth of 985ft (300m).

Left: *Ohio,* the US Navy's first purpose-built Trident missile submarine, immediately before launching ceremony, April 1979.

The eventual number of Trident-carrying SSBNs depends on two principal factors. The first is the outcome of the new round of Strategic Arms Limitation Talks (or Strategic Arms Reduction Talks) between the Reagan administration and the USSR, which will then, of course, have to be ratified by the US Congress. Any such agreement would presumably include, as in SALT-II proposals, the maximum numbers of SLBMs and launch platforms that each super-power was prepared to permit the other to possess. The other factor is the development of new types of long-range cruise missiles, some of which can be used in a strategic role even when launched from a standard 21in (533mm) submerged torpedo tube. This, and similar progress in other fields, may restrict the need for large numbers of SLBMs in huge and very expensive SSBNs. The great advantage, however, of the current generation of very long-range SLBMs is that they can be launched from American or Soviet home waters, thus making detection of the launch platform and destruction of either the submarine or the missiles launched from it extremely difficult, if not virtually impossible.

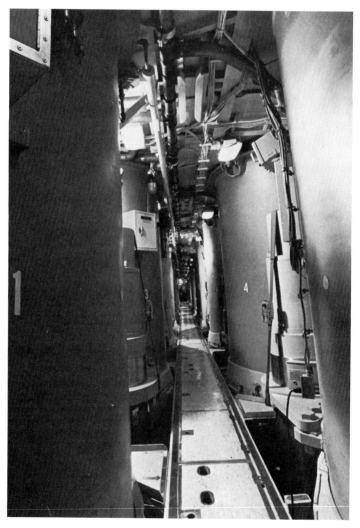

Top: Port bow view of *Ohio* during sea trials in the Atlantic, September 1981. With a submerged displacement of 18,700 tons, *Ohio* is outweighed only by the Soviet Typhoon class.

Above: Early in 1978, *Ohio* is rolled out of the assembly building at General Dynamics (Electric Boat Division) on to a waterfront pier for final assembly and testing.

Left: The ballistic missile compartment (looking towards the bow) of *Ohio,* seen shortly before commissioning in late 1981. An SSBN of the Ohio class—a total of sixteen is now planned—mounts twentyfour tubes for the Trident 1 SLBM.

USS *Ohio* (SSBN-726).

Lafayette Class/Franklin Class

Total built:	31.
Launched:	1962-66.
Status:	31 in service.
Displacement:	7,250 tons (surfaced); 8,250 tons (submerged).
Dimensions:	Length, 425ft (129.5m); beam, 33ft (10.1m); draught, 31ft 6in (9.6m).
Missiles:	16 Poseidon C-3 (19 boats); 16 Trident C-4 (12 boats).
Torpedo tubes:	Four 21in (533mm).
Propulsion:	Nuclear (15,000shp).
Shafts:	One.
Speed:	20kt, 37km/hr (surfaced); 30kt, 55.5km/hr (submerged).
Complement:	Lafayette: 140; Franklin: 168.

The 31 Lafayette class SSBNs were the definitive US submarines of the 1960s and 1970s. The first eight were originally fitted with Polaris A-2 missiles, while the remaining 23 had the improved Polaris A-3 with a range of 2,855 miles (4,594km) and three 200KT MRV warheads. The first five boats launched their missiles with compressed air, but the remainder use a rocket motor to produce a gas-steam mixture to eject the missiles from their tubes. All Lafayettes have now been fitted to take Poseidon C-3 SLBMs, which have a range of about 3,230 miles (5,200km) with ten 50KT MIRVs.

Above right: USS *Lafayette* (SSBN-616) under way on the surface in Hampton Roads, Virginia, December 1968. Laid down in January 1961 and launched in May 1962, *Lafayette* was the first SSBN of this class commissioned, 23 April 1963.

Right: Immediately after commissioning, *Lafayette* cruises on the surface, Long Island Sound. A pressurised-water cooled S5W reactor and two geared turbines, with a single shaft, give the Lafayettes speeds of 20kt surfaced and 30kt submerged.

Below: Lafayette class *John Adams* (SSBN-620) cruises in the Pacific. When refuelled around 1970, these boats received nuclear cores giving enough power for about 400,000 miles.

The Lafayettes are slightly enlarged and improved versions of the Ethan Allen design, and are almost indistinguishable from that class. The last 12 Lafayettes differ considerably from the earlier boats and are sometimes referred to as the Benjamin Franklin class. They have improved, quieter machinery and 28 more crewmen. Twelve of these are being refitted to take the larger three-stage Trident 1 C-4 SLBM, which has a range of about 4,400 miles (7,100km) and carries eight 100KT MIRVs. Although these SSBNs do not have the underwater performance of the SSNs, they have a respectable capability against surface ships or other submarines and are armed with conventional or wire-guided torpedoes and Subroc. Normally, however, they would attempt to evade detection or contact.

Daniel Webster (SSBN-626) of this class has been fitted with diving planes on a raised bow sonar instead of on the fin; although this has been successful, it has not been copied on other SSBNs.

Top: *Benjamin Franklin*
(SSBN-640). The last twelve
Lafayettes, with a larger
complement, are sometimes
designated the Franklin class.

Above left: *Sam Rayburn*
(SSBN-635). Each Lafayette/
Franklin boat carries sixteen
Poseidon C-3 or Trident C-4.

Above: Officer of the deck in
night vision glasses as USS
Francis Scott Key (SSBN-657)
prepares to surface.

Left: Starboard beam view of
Benjamin Franklin cruising in
San Juan Bay, January 1966,
soon after commissioning.

Submarine Launched Strategic Missiles

Perhaps the best way to trace the development of submarine-based strategic missiles is to examine the US Navy sequence: Loon, Triton, Rigel, Regulus, Polaris, Poseidon, Trident and Tomahawk. This appears at first glance to be a circular path, beginning and ending with wings, but, in fact, it is only now being understood in the West that the cruise missile and the ballistic missile are complementary. Unfortunately, the USSR seems to have appreciated this all along.

After the war the Americans studied German records in great detail, especially those concerning advanced projects such as the 'V' weapons. Surprisingly, the German Navy had shown only the most cursory interest in missile projects, and it was left to the US Navy to be the first to try to mate the V-1 flying bomb to a submarine. Under the codename Loon this proved a reasonable success, encouraging the Americans to proceed with further development of the basic concept of the missile.

Guidance is a critical area in missile technology. In the late 1940s it was assumed that the only targets for missiles would be cities, and this assumption allowed for a variety of navigation systems. One such family was based on radio methods: the Rigel and Triton missile systems used an area-coverage hyperbolic method, in which either pulsed or continuous-wave emissions from two fixed stations (radar 'picket' submarines) mutually interacted to generate a fixed pattern of hyperbolic lines down which the missile would guide itself. A totally different method was astro-tracking, in which a gyro-stabilised tracker in the missile locked on to a star or other suitable heavenly body and navigated by a computerised version of the traditional mariners' sextant. This method can achieve great degrees of accuracy, but it has taken many years for it to achieve reliability.

By the mid-1950s the inertial navigation system (INS) was under active development. This measures all accelerations in all three planes experienced by a vehicle and then integrates them with respect to time to give a continuous record of velocity. It then integrates the velocities with respect to time to give a continuous record of position. To do this, the INS must know exactly where it was at the outset. The accelerations are measured by sensitive accelerometers, which are among the most precise engineering achievements to date. Nevertheless, if the start point—in the case of an SLBM, a submerged and moving submarine—is not known to an accuracy of greater than ±50nm, there will be a similar degrading effect on the accuracy at the target. For this reason, SLBMs are targeted in a counter-value role against enemy cities. There is a possibility, however, that Manoeuvrable Re-entry Vehicles (MaRVs) will be able to guide themselves to the precise target, with a CEP of 20 to 40m, entirely by on-board systems, independent of any navigational imprecisions in the submarine. Such a development would enable the SLBM to become a counter-force weapon, and this would change the whole strategic equation.

United States of America

No weapon system in history combined more dramatic technological innovations than the bold concept for a submarine-launched ballistic missile, formed by Admiral W.F. Raborn and a team from Lockheed. Two vital decisions taken at the very start of the project were to use a solid propellant and to blow the missile from a vertical tube while submerged. The Polaris project, however, involved much more than this: it included lightweight

Above: Trident I (C-4) SLBM is test-launched from Lafayette class submarine USS *John C. Calhoun* (SSBN-630), October 1980.

ablative RVs; miniature inertial guidance; miniaturised nuclear and thermonuclear warheads; cold-gas launch techniques; submarine navigation, noise reduction and cavitation. Polaris reached operational status in November 1960 and changed the face of warfare and, in particular, of deterrence.

Naturally, improvement programmes began at once; the Polaris A-1 was succeeded by the A-2 and A-3, before being replaced by the Poseidon, which became operational in March 1971. This, in turn, is now giving way to the Trident, which will be the US Navy's strategic missile through to the 21st century. What is really impressive about the original Polaris programme is that naval officers and scientists in the 1950s got the concept so exactly right: Trident is a totally recognizable descendant of the first SLBM.

Soviet Union

The Soviet SLBM programme began with the SS-N-4 (NATO codename: Serb) in about 1953, possibly antedating the US Navy's initiation of studies for a seagoing Jupiter liquid-fuelled missile. SS-N-4 was probably the first large missile designed to be compatible with a ship, but it was of such a size that it could only just be fitted between the keel of a submarine and the top of its fin. The missile was installed in this fashion in the Zulu V, Golf and Hotel submarines. Next came the SS-N-5, again installed in the fin, although it can be fired submerged.

From a position of technological disadvantage the USSR has gradually attained, first of all, parity and, now, superiority. The SS-N-6 was the first SLBM small enough to avoid the limitations of the fin installation and 12 were mounted

in Yankee class SSBNs. A step further was taken with the SS-N-8, whose range on early tests of 4,847 miles (7,800km) far exceeded that of any other SLBM, but was quickly overtaken by subsequent observations. Both SS-N-6 and SS-N-8 had versions with MRV heads, but it was not until SS-N-8 Mod 3 that the Soviet Navy obtained a true MIRV capability. Further, with the Delta II SSBN they at last equalled the Western ability to mount 16 tubes on the hull of one submarine.

SS-NX-13 was tested in the mid-1970s and caused anxiety in the West because it appeared to be an SS-N-6 operating in the depressed trajectory mode. Not only did this pose strategic problems for the defence of the USA, it also appeared at the time to be a clever method of avoiding some of the prohibitions imposed by the SALT-I

treaty. So far as is known, however, this missile has never attained operational status.

SS-NX-17 was another project which was tested in the 1970s, but which does not seem to have progressed. The latest operational missile is the SS-N-18, which has virtually all the capabilities of the Trident II, but which attained them at least a decade earlier. Its range capability is such that Soviet SSBNs can now threaten the USA from almost any part of any ocean in the world. This process continues with the SS-NX-20, which started tests in 1980. Presumed to be intended for the 25,000-ton Typhoon class SSBN, the SS-NX-20 is known to have encountered many problems during its test programme. This is by no means unique, however: many Western projects have had to overcome early problems and have gone on to achieve great opera-

Above: The first in the sequence of the USN's submarine based strategic missiles. LTV-N-2 Loon (a post-war development of the German "V-1" flying bomb) is fired from an aft-facing ramp on a surfaced submarine off the Naval Air Missile Test Center, Point Mugu, in May 1949.

Far left: Note the absence of the standard flight markings on this Polaris A-3 SLBM fired from the Lafayette class USS *Daniel Webster* (SSBN-626) in 1964, the year in which this missile became operational.

Left: France's current SLBM is the 1,926-mile (3,100km) range MSBS M-20. Here an M-20 test vehicle is seen breaking the surface, almost certainly having been fired from the trials submarine *Gymnote*.

tional successes. If the Soviet Navy has a real need for the SS-NX-20, there can be no doubt that resources will be poured into its development until all problems are satisfactorily resolved.

The overall picture that emerges from the Soviet SLBM story is one of constant and consistent progress. The USSR's goal, it must be presumed, is to bring to bear the maximum threat upon the USA—and in this the Soviets have certainly succeeded.

Other Nations

The French have undertaken their own SLBM programme, following the same general lines of development as the USA but utilising their own national resources. Their missiles are not as technologically advanced as those of the USA and USSR, but they seem to be adequate for France's political and military requirements alike.

The UK uses American missiles, providing only its own 'front-end', ie, RVs, the nuclear devices and penaids. This has enabled the UK to obtain a nuclear deterrent force under its own control at a relatively small cost. Although it is now the only user of Polaris, the UK has updated the warheads and penetration systems, which will maintain the deterrent capability until the arrival of Trident in the early 1990s.

The only other nation in this field is the People's Republic of China. Little is known of her programme, but it is generally assumed that she has at least one Golf class SSB armed with missiles. An explosion aboard such a vessel was reported in the Western press in October 1981. Certainly, China has the technological ability to produce an effective SLBM if she so wishes.

UGM-73 Poseidon C-3

Status:	In service on 19 Franklin and Lafayette class SSBNs, each with 16 tubes.
Dimensions:	Length, 34ft (10.36m); diameter, 74in (188cm).
Launch weight:	About 65,000lb (29,500kg).
Propulsion:	First stage: Thiokol solid motor with gas-pressurised gimballed nozzle. Second stage: Hercules motor with similar type nozzle.
Guidance:	Inertial.
Range:	See **Warhead.**
Warhead:	MIRV system carrying ten 50KT RVs for ultimate range of 3,230 miles (5,200km), or 14 MIRVs for 2,485 miles (4,000km).

Resulting from prolonged studies of the benefits of later technology, Poseidon C-3 was installed in Franklin and Lafayette class SSBNs, starting with USS *James Madison* (SSBN-627). This boat carried out the first Poseidon deployment on 31 March 1971. Compared with Polaris A-3, Poseidon has at least equal range, carried double the payload, and has twice the accuracy (ie, half the Circular Error Probable) as well as much improved MIRV and penaid capability. A modification programme, begun in 1973 to rectify deficiencies which showed up after IOC was achieved in 1970, was completed in 1978. More than 40 missiles withdrawn from submarines after operational patrols have been fired, with excellent results.

Poseidon is currently deployed on the Franklin and Lafayette class SSBNs. All 31 boats were fitted for Poseidon, but under current plans 12 will be converted to take Trident, leaving 19 with Poseidon. This missile system will thus serve until at least the late 1980s.

Above: This Poseidon SLBM, already headed down-range, was fired on the Eastern Test Range by the Lafayette/Franklin boat *George Bancroft* (SSBN-643), 25 September 1972.

Above right: A Poseidon missile is lowered for test-fitting in a launch tube aboard USS *James Madison* (SSBN-627). Inset: *James Madison* with all sixteen missile tubes open; some, with white Styrofoam closures sealed, are loaded.

Right: Missile compartment on USS *John Adams* (SSBN-620), early 1973. All Lafayettes now carry Poseidon C-3 SLBM.

UGM-27 Polaris A-3

Status:	Operational only on four Royal Navy Resolution class SSBNs.
Dimensions:	Length, 31ft 6in (9.6m); diameter, 54in (137cm).
Launch weight:	35,000lb (15,850kg).
Propulsion:	First stage: Aerojet motor with glass-fibre case and four rotatable nozzles. Second stage: Hercules motor with liquid injection.
Guidance:	Inertial.
Range:	2,855 miles (4,595km).
Warhead:	Three British-designed and -made MRV.

Development of the Polaris weapon system began in 1956, when it became apparent that an advanced solid-propulsion missile to fit submarine launch tubes was viable. This would, of course, permit the missile to be carried much closer to its target, and would also enable the launch platform to remain hidden in the depths of the ocean. UGM-27, Polaris A-1, became operational on the first US Fleet Ballistic Missile System (FBMS) submarine in 1960, only five years after the first nuclear-powered submarine, USS *Nautilus,* had made its maiden voyage. In 1962 the first live test of the missile from an operational submarine resulted in an impact precisely on the target. None of this version remains in use.

UGM-27B, Polaris A-2, had a longer second stage which resulted in increased range, and became operational in 1962. None remains operational, but many are in use in test programmes.

Polaris A-3 achieved a 60 per cent increase in range by filling the available space more efficiently, as well as using a lighter structure and a better propellant. Operational since 1964, it remains in use only on the four British boats of the Resolution class. The British Polaris A-3 missiles are each fitted with three 200KT MRV warheads of British design, in re-entry vehicles which are also of British origin. Various proposals to replace the Polaris A-3 have been rejected for financial or political reasons, but the effectiveness of the force has been maintained by an interim programme codenamed 'Chevaline'. This has upgraded the missiles through improvements to the RVs and warheads, and advanced penetration aids have been installed. The programme has cost about £1 billion and will maintain the effectiveness of the British strategic deterrent until the late 1990s, despite known improvements to Soviet ABM systems.

Below: First submerged firing of Polaris A-1, 20 July 1960.

UGM-93 Trident C-4

Status:	First deployment has commenced: 12 Franklin/Lafayette class converted to take Trident; 16 Ohio class planned. UK has also ordered Trident.
Dimensions:	Length, 34ft (10.36m); diameter, 74in (188cm).
Launch weight:	70,000lb (32,000kg).
Propulsion:	Three tandem stages; advanced solid motors with thrust vectoring.
Guidance:	Inertial.
Range:	4,400 miles (7100km).
Warhead:	Eight Mark 4 100KT MIRV. Mark 500 Evader MaRV may be installed later.

Some 16 extremely large submarines of the Ohio class, each boat mounting 24 launch tubes, are projected to carry this large, long-range SLBM system. Flight testing of the Trident I (C-4) missile improved after a somewhat shaky start and the system is now operational. Trident I (C-4) will be installed in 12 units of the Franklin/Lafayette class and the first such conversion, USS *Francis Scott Key* (SSBN-657), has joined the fleet as the first operational Trident-armed submarine. Trident II (D-5), a longer missile which would have much improved throw-weight and/or range, is currently the subject of much discussion. It would fit the C-4 launch tubes for diameter, but, being somewhat longer, would not only need new tubes but also a new submarine launch platform.

The British Government has announced plans to purchase Trident missiles, which will be installed in a new class of British-built SSBNs. As with Polaris, an entirely British front-end will be fitted, thus ensuring ultimate national control over deployment and targeting. A final decision on whether to buy the C-4 or to go straight to the D-5 has yet to be made.

Above: Shakedown operation launch of Trident from *John C. Calhoun* (SSBN-630) off Florida, 28 October 1980.

Left: Launch of Trident 1 (C-4), now becoming operational in Lafayette/Franklin class SSBNs.

MSBS M-20/MSBS M-4

Status: M-20: in service in five Le Redoutable class SSBNs;
M-4: under development for deployment
in seven SSBNs in mid-1980s.

Dimensions: M-20: length, 34ft 1½in (10.4m); diameter,
59in (150cm).
M-4: length, 36ft 1in (11m); diameter, 75³/₅in
(192cm).

Launch weight: M-20: 44,091lb (20,000kg);
M-4: 79,365lb (36,000kg).

Propulsion: M-20: two-stage, solid fuel; thrust vector control.
M-4: three-stage, solid fuel; first and second stage
have mechanical steering, third has thrust vector
control.

Guidance: M-20/M-4: inertial.

Range: M-20: 1,926 miles (3,100km);
M-4: 2,485 miles (4,000km).

Warhead: M-20: MR-61 with one 1MT weapon;
M-4: six MIRV, each of 150KT yield.

Mer-Sol Ballistique Strategique (MSBS) is the French national strategic nuclear deterrent. It was broadly based on the Polaris concept, but has been achieved with little non-French help other than the licensing of essential technology. The early test vehicles flew between 1967 and 1970 and led to the MSBS M-1, which entered service in *Le Redoutable* in December 1971. The M-1 had a single warhead with a yield of 500KT and a range of 1,491 miles (2,400km). This was followed by the M-2 which had a new second stage and a range increased to 1,926 miles (3,100km). The M-2 was installed in *Le Foudroyant* during construction and was retrofitted to the earlier boats during the course of refits.

The current missile system is the M-20, standard on the five operational Sousmarin Nucleaire Lanceur d'Engins (SNLE). This is generally similar to M-2, but has a more powerful warhead with advanced penetration aids.

For the second half of the 1980s a completely new M-4 missile is being developed, which has very little in common with earlier French MSBS. It can, however, be fitted into the existing submarines after considerable modifications. It has a three-stage propulsion system and will mount six MIRVs, each with a yield of approximately 150KT. Flight testing has already begun and an IOC around 1985 is envisaged. Like the SSBN (SNLE) programme, the development and fielding of an entirely French strategic nuclear missile system is a truly remarkable national achievement.

**Above right: Submarine launch of France's MSBS M-20
SLBM, which has a range of 1,926 miles (3,100km).**

**Right: The French Navy's trials submarine *Gymnote* is fitted
with a mass model of the MSBS M-4 SLBM at Cherbourg Arsenal.**

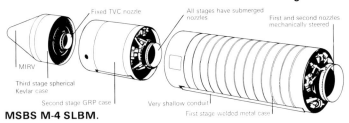

MSBS M-4 SLBM.

SS-N-6 Mod 3

Status:	In service in 28 Yankee I class SSBNs.
Dimensions:	Length, 31ft 8in (9.65m); diameter, 64.9in (165cm).
Launch weight:	44,000lb (19,958kg).
Propulsion:	Two-stage, liquid fuel.
Guidance:	Inertial.
Range:	1,864 miles (3,000km).
Warhead:	Two 350KT MRV.
CEP:	1.0nm (1,850m).

This third-generation SLBM shows a totally fresh Soviet approach, and when it was first seen in the November 1967 parade it posed several problems to Western observers. Geometrically superior to SS-N-5, it has the optimum shape to fill a launch-tube. At first thought to have solid-fuel propulsion, it is now believed to have storable liquid, almost certainly N_2O_4/UDMH. The first stage is large, accounting for almost 75 per cent of the launch weight, with four vectored nozzles. There is no cold expulsion device attached to the missile; this must be part of the launch installation in the Yankee I class SSBNs which have carried SS-N-6 since its IOC in 1967.

It would appear that the SS-N-6/Yankee combination was the first the USSR deemed worthy of an all-out effort, and from 1966 eight Yankees a year were produced, until superseded by the Delta I. A total of 33 was produced.

Three versions of SS-N-6 are known in the West, and are believed to be interchangeable. SS-N-6 Mod 1, the original type, had a warhead estimated as having a 1 to 2MT yield. SS-N-6 Mod 2, seen on test in 1972 and deployed from 1973, had improved propulsion giving a substantial increase in range. The US DoD has stated that Mod 2 could hit any part of the USA from the 100 fathom (600ft, 183m) line. Mod 3, which followed closely after Mod 2, has two MRVs which are not independently targetable. According to the DoD, Mod 3 still does not have a hard-target capability. It is estimated that all SS-N-6 now deployed are the Mod 3 version.

SS-NX-17

Status:	Tested on the single Yankee II in 1977-79.
Dimensions:	Length, 36ft 4in (11.1m); diameter, 65in (165cm).
Launch weight:	Not known.
Propulsion:	Two-stage, solid fuel, with Post Boost Vehicle.
Guidance:	Inertial.
Range:	2,763 miles (4,446km).
Warhead:	1MT.

This is believed to be the first Soviet SLBM to use solid propellant. Prototypes were seen on flight test from land sites in 1975 and testing at sea began in 1977-78 in the specially-constructed Yankee II SSBN. The missile is reported to be a two-stage device with a Post Boost Vehicle, the first on a Soviet SLBM. Surprisingly, the only test observations have detected the use of only one warhead. The dimensions published to date do not seem to make SS-NX-17 compatible with existing Delta or Yankee launch tubes, and it may be that the missile is, or was, intended for another type of submarine.

SS-N-8

Status:	In service in eighteen Delta I and four Delta II SSBNs.
Dimensions:	Length, 42ft 6in (12.95m); diameter, 79in (200cm).
Launch weight:	45,000lb (20,412kg).
Propulsion:	Two-stage, storable liquid.
Guidance:	Stellar-inertial.
Range:	4,846 miles (7,800km).
Warhead:	One 800KT.
CEP:	0.84nm (1,550m).

In 1971 this missile began an apparently extremely successful flight test programme from a single rebuilt Hotel III SSBN. The SS-N-8 quickly demonstrated a range of 4,846 miles (7,800km), which the then Chairman of the Joint Chiefs of Staff said exceeded by at least 1,864 miles (3,000km) the range of any other existing SLBM. It introduced "a totally new problem" into Western defence planning—and the impact of subsequent tests, when the missile showed ranges exceeding 5,717 miles (9,200km), can thus be imagined. SS-N-8 apparently outperforms Trident I, and the latter is only just entering service with the US Navy.

SS-N-8 is believed to be a two-stage missile with storable liquid propellant and a stellar-inertial navigation system (unique in a ballistic missile) which gives a CEP of about 0.84nm (1,550m). Somewhat larger than SS-N-6, the SS-N-8 needed the largest submarines ever built (until then) to carry it—the Delta I class. Even with a hull diameter at least as large as on the Yankee class, the missile length is such that the launch tubes project well above the hull casing. The Delta I class carried twelve SS-N-8, but the Soviet Navy, determined to match Western SSBNs, created the Delta II by inserting an extra 55ft (17m) section, thus permitting carriage of sixteen SLBMs. So far as is known, only the Mod 1 version of SS-N-8 has entered service.

SS-N-18 Mod 1

Status:	Operational on at least eleven Delta III SSBN.
Dimensions:	Length, 46ft 4in (14.1m); diameter, 71in (180cm).
Launch weight:	44,000lb (19,958kg).
Propulsion:	Two-stage, liquid fuel, with Post Boost Vehicle.
Guidance:	Stellar-inertial.
Range:	5,988 miles (9,635km).
Warhead:	Three 200KT MIRV.
CEP:	0.76nm (1410m).

The most recent Soviet SLBM to become operational, the SS-N-18 was first seen on test flights some weeks after testing had begun on the SS-NX-17. It is now fully deployed on Delta III submarines and has sufficient range for the launch vehicles to be able to operate from havens in the Barents Sea and the Sea of Okhotsk. Two developments of the original type have been identified, but whether they are yet deployed is uncertain. The Mod 2 has one 450KT warhead and a range of 4,970 miles (8,000km), while the Mod 3 has no less than seven MIRVs and a range of 5,750 miles (9,250km). This is a most formidable missile by any standard.

Cruise Missile Submarines and Submarine Launched Cruise Missiles

The development of submarine launched cruise missiles (SLCM) and the boats to carry them (SSGs) stretches back some 35 years. However, the only two nations really involved—the USA and USSR—have had totally different requirements and as a result have followed quite separate paths.

United States of America

The US Navy initiated its first SLCM programme in 1946 with the Rigel, a supersonic ramjet-powered missile. Launched from a surfaced submarine it could deliver a 3,000lb (1,361kg) HE or nuclear warhead at Mach 2 out to a range of 576 miles (927km). Another system was Triton, again ramjet powered, which featured inertial guidance with radar monitoring and "map matching to refine the guidance and allow the use of a low yield warhead", an extraordinarily advanced concept for its day. These two projects were cancelled in 1952 and 1955 respectively.

In parallel was Regulus, a much less ambitious system based on the German V-1, which had been tested on US submarines in the late 1940s. Regulus I was powered by a turbojet fed through a nose intake and had a range of some 400 miles (644km). A number entered service and were deployed from 1959 to 1964 on USS *Growler* and *Grayback* (two missiles each) and on USS *Halibut*, which was nuclear-powered and mounted five missiles.

The much more advanced Regulus II was larger and was fitted with inertial guidance. It could deliver a nuclear warhead to ranges exceeding 1,000 miles (1,609km) at speeds of Mach 2+. This system was to have replaced Regulus I on *Grayback, Growler, Halibut* and two other submarines, but was cancelled in 1959 just as deployment was about to begin.

In all these cases the missiles were stored in a large circular hangar mounted abaft the fin. To launch, the hangar door had to be opened, the missile moved out onto the end of a launching rail, and wings and tail surfaces fitted. This must have been a fairly lengthy proceeding, but the threat to surfaced submarines was perhaps not quite so acute in those days. The advent of Polaris put an end to the early US SLCM programmes and the submarines concerned were converted to other uses. Then, after a gap of a decade, development of the US Navy's Tomahawk began in 1974. This exists in two versions: one for land attack with Tercom guidance and a nuclear warhead; the other for anti-shipping missions with an HE warhead. Specifically designed to fit a standard 21in (533mm) torpedo tube, Tomahawk does not, like previous SLCMs, need a specially-designed SSG to carry it.

Soviet Union

The Soviet cruise missile submarines were conceived in the 1950s as an answer to the threat from NATO carrier task groups. Some crude conversions of Whiskey class boats were undertaken, but the first major classes to be designed for the purpose were the nuclear-powered Echo class and their diesel-engined counterparts the Juliett class. The Echo class was adapted from the November class SSNs and the first models (Echo I) carried six SS-N-3 missiles. These boats were soon superseded by the larger Echo II design with eight missiles; 29 of these are in service. Only 16 Julietts, an adaptation of the Foxtrot class patrol submarines, were built. In both Echo and Juliett classes, the SS-N-3 is mounted in a bin stowed flush with the hull casing, which is raised prior to firing. There are prominent indentations behind each launcher

Above: US-developed Harpoon anti-submarine missile test-fired from Valiant class HMS *Churchill*, April 1980. This ASM has been ordered for the Royal Navy's nuclear-powered submarines.

which act as blast deflectors—and which generate very considerable underwater noise.

Most, if not all, Julietts serve with the Northern Fleet, while the Echo IIs are divided more or less evenly between Northern and Pacific Fleets. The reason for this may be that the greater endurance of the Echo is regarded as essential to anti-carrier operations in the Pacific; which, in turn, suggests that the Julietts in the Northern Fleet would deploy closer to their home bases. Certainly, their relatively quiet diesel-electric propulsion system is better employed on patrols in the line of advance of the NATO carrier forces; they are, in any case, too slow to try to hunt

down the carriers. Julietts are also frequently deployed to the Mediterranean, where their small size and quieter operation gives them an advantage over the Echo class.

The major weakness of both submarines lies in the nature of the missile they carry. Not only does it have to be fired from the surface, inviting detection and attack, but it also requires target data and midcourse guidance from an external source, usually an aircraft, if it is to attain its maximum range. If the target is a carrier, it is highly unlikely that it would allow reconnaissance aircraft to supply data to the submarine or its missile. Only in a very confused tactical situation would such a manoeuvre be prac-

Above: The anti-shipping Tomahawk SLCM was specifically designed to fit a standard 21in (533mm) torpedo tube.

Above right: Soviet Echo II SSGN; note foremost of the four starboard bins for SS-N-3 or SS-N-12 (Sandbox) launchers.

ticable. However, these older Soviet SSGN/SSGs remain useful against lesser targets in open ocean operations, and also have a significant capability against land targets. The SS-N-3 packs a powerful punch and can carry either a conventional or a nuclear warhead.

The majority of the Charlie class boats serve with the Northern Fleet, with one or two units in the Pacific Fleet. This class, which first appeared in 1968, is a second-generation SSGN, and a significant improvement on the earlier Echo, being smaller, quieter and faster. Most important, however, is the SS-N-7 SLCM, of which eight are carried in launch tubes set into the bow casing and covered by hatches. SS-N-7 is a short-range (28 miles, 45km) anti-ship missile which can be fired while the submarine is submerged. It does not need a relay aircraft and can be fired on the basis of information from the submarine's own sensors. The later Charlie boats have a lengthened bow section, suggesting that they are also fitted to carry and launch the SS-N-15 anti-submarine missile.

The latest Soviet SSGN—the 18,000-ton Oscar—was launched in 1980, and indicates that the Soviet Navy is pursuing this line of development. Its 24 missiles, launched from underwater, are similar in concept to the US Tomahawk in its anti-shipping role, but are strictly tactical in application.

SSGN Operations

It would be easier to defend against the SSGN submarine than against the missile. An important NATO countermeasure would be to have SSNs precede a task group, clearing SSGN/SSG as they go. Soviet SSGN/SSG directed to intercept from other positions would have to move at high speed, and would therefore expose themselves to detection by passive sonar or hydrophone arrays. ASW aircraft such as S-3 Viking, Nimrod or Atlantique could then be directed to the spot to kill or deter the SSGN/SSG. Such actions should be relatively easy in the case of older boats such as the Echo and Juliett because of their noisy propulsion system and strange hull-form. Even the newer Charlie boats have free-flood holes in their casings and their propulsion systems are still noisier than their NATO counterparts.

Perhaps the most effective area of operations for Soviet SSGN/SSG is the Norwegian Sea, where general conditions and the proximity of their home bases would enable them to mount heavy attacks on NATO task groups operational in that location.

Whiskey Twin Cylinder Class/ Whiskey Long-Bin Class/ Juliett Class

Total built/ converted:	Whiskey Twin Cylinder: 5; Whiskey Long-Bin: 6; Juliett: 16.
Launched/ converted:	Whiskey Twin Cylinder: 1958-60; Whiskey Long-Bin: 1960-63; Juliett: 1961-66.
Status:	Whiskey Twin Cylinder: 2 in service; Whiskey Long-Bin: 3 in service; Juliett: 16 in service.
Displacement:	Whiskey Twin Cylinder: 1,050 tons (surfaced), 1,400 tons (submerged); Whiskey Long-Bin 1,200 tons (surfaced), 1,500 tons (submerged); Juliett: 3,000 tons (surfaced), 3,700 tons (submerged).
Dimensions:	Whiskey Twin Cylinder: length, 249ft 4in (76m); beam, 21ft 4in (6.5m); draught: 16ft 5in (5m). Whiskey Long-Bin: length, 274ft 11in (83.8m); beam, 21ft 4in (6.5m); draught, 16ft 5in (5m). Juliett: length, 284ft 5in (86.7m); beam, 33ft 1in (10.1m); draught, 22ft 11in (7m).
Missiles:	Whiskey Twin Cylinder: two SS-N-3; Whiskey Long-Bin: four SS-N-3; Juliett: four SS-N-3A.
Torpedo tubes:	Whiskey Twin Cylinder: six 21in (533mm); Whiskey Long-Bin: four 21in (533mm); Juliett: six 21in (533mm).
Propulsion:	Whiskey Twin Cylinder/Whiskey Long-Bin: diesel, two (4,000bhp); electric, two (2,700shp). Juliett: diesel, three (7,000bhp); electric, three (5,000shp).
Shafts:	Whiskey Twin Cylinder/Long-Bin/Juliett: two.
Speed:	Whiskey Twin Cylinder: 18kt, 33km/hr (surfaced), 13kt, 24km/hr (submerged); Whiskey Long-Bin 18kt, 33km/hr (surfaced), 12kt, 22km/hr (submerged); Juliett: 19kt, 35km/hr (surfaced), 17kt, 31.5km/hr (submerged).
Complement:	Whiskey Twin Cylinder: 56; Whiskey Long-Bin: 60; Juliett: 79.

The earliest Soviet experiments with an SS-N-3 (Shaddock) SLCM involved one launcher mounted on the casing of an otherwise unmodified Whiskey class conventional patrol submarine (Whiskey Single Cylinder). This was followed in 1958-60 by a twin missile installation (Whiskey Twin Cylinder): five boats were thus converted. A crude and obviously hasty conversion, it is rather surprising that two remain in service, but they are presumably only used for training.

Whiskey Twin Cylinder SSG.

Top: The pair of launchers that give the class its name are clearly seen in this photograph of a Soviet Whiskey Twin Cylinder cruise missile submarine under way. This crude conversion allowed a conventional patrol submarine to carry two SS-N-3 (Shaddock) SLCMs abaft the fin. Five boats were converted in 1958-1960, of which two are still in service.

Above: Even dressed overall for review, little can improve the appearance of the Whiskey Long-Bin SSG, with its bulky fin redesigned to accommodate four SS-N-3 launchers. Although an improvement on the Twin Cylinder, the Long-Bin is very noisy when submerged and of limited operational value.

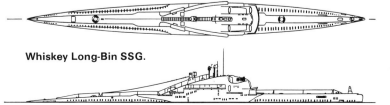

Whiskey Long-Bin SSG.

The next step in the evolution of an effective SSG was the Whiskey Long-Bin, in which four SS-N-3 launchers were mounted in a re-designed and rather monstrous fin. The hull was lengthened by some 25ft 7in (7.8m) to accommodate this. Although something of an improvement on the Whiskey Twin Cylinder, the Whiskey Long-Bin too is both noisy and of limited operational value.

Although they represented a great advance on the crude conversions of the Whiskey class, the excellent Julietts were in turn overtaken by the bigger and heavier-armed Echo class (or, it may be that they were designed as a safeguard against failure of the then new nuclear propulsion systems). Nevertheless, the Julietts are nimble and very much cheaper than the Echo class and 16 were commissioned between 1962 and 1966. They are well equipped with sonar and communications and have proved very successful. The Julietts are essentially Foxtrots with an enlarged hull incorporating hydraulically-elevated missile tubes derived from the Whiskey class conversions. Many Julietts, nearly all with minor individual differences in equipment, are seen regularly in the Mediterranean and Atlantic.

Above right: With four hydraulically-elevated launch tubes for the SS-N-3A missile, the Juliett class proved far more effective than the Whiskey conversions that preceded them.

Below: A Juliett SSG under way. Although to some extent superseded by the more powerful Echo class, all sixteen Julietts commissioned in 1962-1966 are still in service.

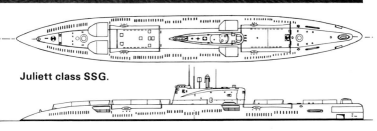

Juliett class SSG.

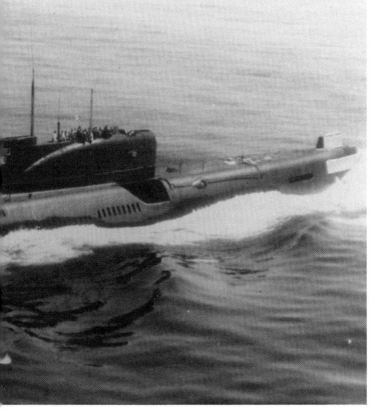

Echo II Class

Total built:	29.
Launched:	1963-69.
Status:	29 in service.
Displacement:	4,800 tons (surfaced); 5,800 tons (submerged).
Dimensions:	Length, 384ft 8ins (117.3m); beam, 30ft 2in (9.2m); draught, 25ft 6in (7.8m).
Missiles:	Eight SS-N-3 or eight SS-N-12 (Sandbox).
Torpedo tubes:	Six 21in (533mm) bow; two 16in (406mm) stern.
Propulsion:	Nuclear (22,500shp).
Shafts:	Two.
Speed:	25kt, 46km/hr (submerged).
Complement:	100.

These large and formidable SSGNs have for many years formed an important part of the Soviet Navy's offensive firepower at sea. Forming a natural follow-on to the Juliett class, they have bigger hulls, generally similar to those of the November class SSNs, and are probably powered by the same 22,500shp nuclear installation (which was the first of its kind to be developed in the USSR).

Top: Under US Navy observation an Echo II SSGN submerges. Boats of this class must surface in order to launch and control their missiles.

Above: Surfacing at evening on 19 September 1973, this damaged Echo II SSGN was located by a Cornwall-based Nimrod aircraft of the RAF.

Left: An Echo II SSGN is tied up alongside a Soviet submarine depot ship. Note the large, uncovered wells housing the missile tubes.

The first five boats—Echo I class—were equipped with three pairs of SS-N-3 launch tubes, but these were later removed and the boats are now used as SSNs. A decision to lengthen the hull and to incorporate a fourth pair of launch tubes resulted in the Echo II class, the first of which appeared in 1962-63. The 29 boats of this class have since been seen in many parts of the world, operating with both the Northern and Pacific Fleets. They have, indeed, achieved some notoriety: on several occasions they have had to surface after accidents and have been towed home.

The Echo II must surface to launch and control its missiles. The tubes are elevated to about 60° for firing, with the large open wells diverting the rocket efflux outboard. Guidance radar is housed in the top forepart of the fin; the casing opens to expose the antenna. A further antenna mast at the after end of the fin is hinged and stowed in a recess in the deck when not required. It seems odd that the Soviet Navy has not devised some form of cover for the large wells, which cause a great deal of noise when the boat is submerged.

Above: Close amidships view
of an Echo II clearly shows
the recess in the casing that
houses the hinged radar aerial
at the after end of the fin.

Left: Five Echo I class boats
remain in service as SSNs—as
seen here—with the original
armament of three pairs of
SS-N-3 launch tubes removed.

Below left: Damaged Echo II
SSGN *(see page 55, above)*
seen in the North Atlantic,
north-west of the Hebrides, by
an RAF Nimrod on 19
September 1973, is now
limping homeward on the
surface. The Echo IIs have
achieved some notoriety
as being accident-prone.

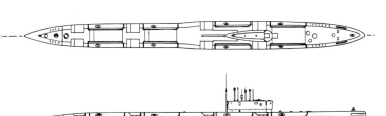

Above: Side view of Echo I SSN (upper) and side and deck
views of Echo II SSGN (lower). In the Echo II design,
the hull was lengthened by some 5ft (1.5m).

Charlie Class

Total built:	Charlie I: 11; Charlie II: 5+.
Launched:	Charlie I: 1967-?; Charlie II: 1973-?
Status:	Charlie I: 11 in service; Charlie II: 5+ in service.
Displacement:	Charlie I: 4,000 tons (surfaced), 4,900 tons (submerged);
	Charlie II: 4,400 tons (surfaced), 5,500 tons (submerged).
Dimensions:	Charlie I: length, 308ft (93.9m); beam, 32ft 6in (9.9m); draught, 24ft 7in (7.5m).
	Charlie II: length, 337ft 6in (102.9m); beam, 32ft 6in (9.9m); draught, 25ft 7in (7.8m).
Missiles:	Charlie I: eight SS-N-7;
	Charlie II: eight SS-N-7 *or* eight SS-N-9 (*see text*).
Torpedo tubes:	Charlie I/II: six 21in (533mm).
Propulsion:	Charlie I/II: nuclear (30,000shp).
Shafts:	Charlie I/II: one.
Speed:	Charlie I/II: 28kt, 52km/hr (submerged).
Complement:	90.

The shortcomings of the Echo class were readily apparent to the Soviet Navy and the next class of SSGN—the Charlie class—has largely rectified those faults. Although the Charlies are still noisier than foreign nuclear submarines, they are a great improvement on the Echos, with much the same hull form and machinery as the Victor I class SSN and a similar high speed. They are fitted with eight missile tubes on the bow casing for SS-N-7 cruise missiles. These have a range of about 28nm (52km) and do not require mid-course guidance from another ship or from an aircraft. They can also be launched while the submarine is submerged, thus greatly decreasing chances of the boat being detected.

Right: Charlie class SSGN, with eight bow-mounted missile tubes.

Below right: Charlie is shadowed by US Navy patrol aircraft.

Below: Charlie class under way in South China Sea, April 1974.

Charlie II is an enlarged version with improved capabilities. Some reports suggest that a new cruise missile may be mounted: the SS-N-9, with a range of more than 60nm (111km), ie, more than double that of the SS-N-7. It is also possible that the SS-N-15, a Subroc type missile, may be fired from the torpedo tubes. Both these types, especially Charlie II, pose a significant threat to NATO surface groups.

Top: Charlie I class SSGN seen by RAF patrol in May 1974.

Above: Amidships view of Charlie class from US Navy aircraft.

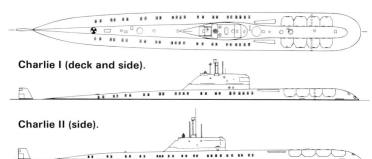

Charlie I (deck and side).

Charlie II (side).

Papa Class/Oscar Class

Total built:	Papa: 1; Oscar 1 (+?).
Launched:	Papa: 1972; Oscar: 1980-?
Status:	Papa: 1 in service; Oscar: trials.
Displacement:	Papa: 5,500 tons (surfaced), 6,500 tons (submerged);
	Oscar: 15,000 tons (surfaced), 18,000 tons (submerged).
Dimensions:	Papa: length, 357ft 6in (109m); beam 37ft 8in (11.5m); draught, 24ft 11in (7.6m).
	Oscar: length, 520ft (158.5m); beam, 60ft (18.3m); draught, 36ft (11m).
Missiles:	Papa: ten SS-N-9 *(see text)*;
	Oscar: twenty-four SS-N-19.
Torpedo tubes:	Papa: six 21in (533mm);
	Oscar: eight 21in (533mm).
Propulsion:	Papa: nuclear (39,000shp);
	Oscar: nuclear (120,000shp).
Shafts:	Papa/Oscar: two.
Speed:	Papa: 30kt, 55.5km/hr (submerged);
	Oscar: 30 (+?)kt, 55.5km/hr (submerged).
Complement:	Papa: 90; Oscar: 130.

The Papa class SSGN was first observed by the West in 1973 and, so far as is known, only one example has been built. It appears to be a development of the Charlie class, but slightly larger and with a more angular fin, flatter top profile, and square covers on the missile tubes. It may have been built as a general trials and development boat (like the French *Gymnote*), or specifically as part of the development programme for the Oscar class. The missile covers suggest that the armament is not the SS-N-7, but there is no confirmation to date as to whether SS-N-9 or SS-N-19 is fitted.

The Papa class SSGN is fitted with six 21in (533mm) torpedo tubes in the bow, and it is possible also that it may carry the SS-N-15. This missile, an anti-submarine weapon with a nuclear warhead and a maximum range estimated at around 29 miles (64km), is reported to have been operational from 1974 onward in Soviet submarines of the Charlie II, Victor II and Tango classes.

The year 1980 saw the launching of two Soviet giants: the Typhoon class SSBN (described elsewhere) and the Oscar class SSGN. The 18,000-ton Oscar is armed with no less than twentyfour SS-N-19, an anti-ship missile capable of being launched from underwater. With a submerged speed probably in excess of 30 knots, an Oscar class SSGN could operate as the advance guard of a task group, capable of attacking major surface combatants out to a range of 200-250 miles (320-400km). Its large missile armament suggests that such an attack might be launched with several missiles, with the intention of overwhelming the task group defences.

Below: Side plan of Papa class SSGN. Note the angularity of the fin as compared with that of the Charlie class (facing page) from which the Papa appears to have been developed.

BGM-109 Tomahawk

Status:	First deployment of 700-mile (1,126km) conventionally-armed version on Los Angeles class SSNs in January 1982; 1,367 mile (2,200km) nuclear version will be deployed on US SSNs in mid-1984.
Dimensions:	Length, 18ft 3in (5.56m); diameter, 21in (53.3cm); wingspan, 8ft 4in (254cm).
Launch weight:	Approximately 4,000lb (1,814kg).
Propulsion:	Williams Research F107 turbofan; 600lb (272kg) static thrust.
Guidance:	McDonnell Douglas Tercom and inertial.
Range:	Initial version, 700 miles (1,126km).
Flight speed:	Mach 0.72 (550mph, 885km/hr, approx).
Warhead:	Conventional or thermonuclear.

Development of the BGM-109 Tomahawk began in December 1972 when the US Navy ordered studies of a Sea-Launched Cruise Missile (SLCM). General Dynamics won the definitive prime contract in March 1976, by which time the programme had broadened to include tactical and strategic versions to be launched from a wide range of platforms. The great significance of the submarine-launched version is that it can be launched from a standard 21in (533mm) torpedo tube; thus, the US Navy does not need the specialized SSGs which the Soviet Navy is currently compelled to produce.

The protocol to the SALT II treaty banned the deployment of cruise missiles with a range greater than 373 miles (600km), but because the US Senate failed to ratify SALT II, the protocol expired on 31 December 1981. Deployment of the initial version of Tomahawk therefore began in January 1982. It has a conventional warhead, a range of some 700 miles (1,126km), and is primarily a land-attack missile. A second, submarine-launched, version will deploy in mid-1982; this is an anti-ship missile with a 250-mile (400km) range. The shorter range is mainly due to a larger warhead and more bulky guidance system. Finally, in mid-1984, the nuclear warhead version will be deployed; with a range of 1,367 miles (2,200km), this will be capable of engaging targets deep inside the USSR.

This unique and very flexible weapon system will add an entirely new capability to the US Navy's submarine fleet, and is already causing considerable concern to the Soviet political and military leadership.

Right: Launched from a torpedo tube on the submerged USS _Barb_ (SSN-596), Tomahawk SLCM surfaces (inset) and heads down-range.

Below: Land-attack version of Tomahawk on test, June 1978. First deployment of submarine-launched version began in 1982.

ASM/USA

RGM-84A Harpoon

Status:	Operational with US Navy submarines since July 1977: 25 SSNs currently equipped; aim is to equip all SSNs by mid-1987. Ordered by 12 overseas navies; deliveries to Royal Navy in 1981-82.
Dimensions:	Length, 15ft 2in (4.62m); diameter, 13.5in (34.3cm); wingspan, 36in (91.4cm).
Launch weight:	1,470lb (667kg).
Propulsion:	Teledyne CAE J402-CA-400 turbojet, 660lb (300kg) static thrust; Aerojet solid boost motor for launch and acceleration.
Guidance:	Pre-launch: parent platform target data and IBM computer. Mid-flight: Lear Siegler strap-down platform and radio altimeter. Terminal: TO active radar seeker.
Range:	Approximately 70 miles (113km).
Flight speed:	Approximately Mach 0.85 (645mph, 1,037km/hr).
Warhead:	500lb (227kg) blast type.

This important weapon system began in 1968 as an ASM project, but three years later was combined with a proposal for a ship- and submarine-launched missile. Harpoon makes maximum use of existing hardware, such as ship fire control systems, submarine launch tubes, etc. The missile is fired from a submarine in a buoyant capsule which breaks up on reaching the surface, where an Aerojet solid-fuel boost motor accelerates it to Mach 0.75 in 2.5 seconds. Flight control is by cruciform rear fins and a radar altimeter holds the desired sea-skimming height; no link with the parent ship is necessary. Approaching the target, an active radar-seeker searches, locks-on and finally directs a pull-up and swoop on to the target from above.

By the end of 1981 more than 2,000 missiles had been ordered by the US Navy and some twelve overseas customers—including the Royal Navy, which intends to arm all its SSNs with Harpoon. Like Tomahawk, Harpoon uses the existing torpedo tube and does not need a specially-developed submarine launch platform.

Above: The buoyant capsule in which it was launched from the standard torpedo tube of a submerged US Navy SSN has broken up on surfacing and the Harpoon ASM accelerates down-range.

SLCM/USSR

SS-N-7 Siren

Status:	In service on Soviet Charlie class SSGNs.
Dimensions:	Length, 22ft (6.7m); diameter, 21.5in (55cm); wingspan, not known.
Launch weight:	Not known.
Propulsion:	Solid fuel rocket motor.
Guidance:	Autopilot; active radar homing.
Range:	62 miles (100km).
Flight speed:	Mach 0.9.
Warhead:	Nuclear 200KT, or 1,100lb (500kg) HE.

So far as is known this missile is carried only by Charlie class SSGNs, although it is possible that it is carried also by the Papa class. The missile is contained in a launcher which is fitted flush with the deck: the launcher can be elevated and the missile launched while under water. The SS-N-7 SLCM appears to be capable of attacking ship targets out to a range estimated at some 62 miles (100km).

SS-N-3 Shaddock

Status: In service in Whiskey Twin Cylinder, Whiskey Long-Bin, Echo II and Juliett classes.
Dimensions: Length, 42ft 8in (13m); diameter, 39in (99cm); wingspan, 6ft 10in (2.1m).
Launch weight: About 9,920lb (4,500kg).
Propulsion: Turbojet or ramjet sustainer.
Guidance: Various types fitted.
Range: Maximum 124 miles (200km) in submarine-launched version.
Flight speed: Mach 1 to Mach 1.4.
Warhead: Believed to be nuclear with kiloton yield.

Although flight tested as long ago as 1954-57, SS-N-3 is a formidable weapon which even today could deliver a crushing blow over great distances. The large body has a pointed nose and an internal turbojet or ramjet sustainer. Underneath are two solid boost motors which are jettisoned after burn-out, at which point the short-span wings deploy. There is a ventral fin, but no horizontal tail surfaces. SS-N-3 exists in numerous sub-types, launched from ships and submarines.

Several of the earliest installations were aboard submarines and in their haste to deploy this missile the Soviet planners, with total disregard for cost, quickly brought into service a variety of launch platforms. The first was the Whiskey Twin Cylinder, with two launch tubes in an elevating frame on the rear deck casing, followed by the equally odd Whiskey Long-Bin conversion. The first custom-built submarines were the Juliett boats, each with a much better installation of two twin launchers which could be elevated from a flush position in the decking. The final scheme was seen in the Echo I class nuclear boats, with three such twin launchers, and the 29 Echo IIs, with four twin launchers. None of these SSGN/SSG carries suitable guidance equipment: it has been assumed that mid-course guidance for the missiles is provided by attendant aircraft.

Below: SS-N-3 Shaddock cruise missiles in their launch tubes in an elevating frame on the after casing of a Soviet Whiskey Twin Cylinder SSG, a converted Whiskey patrol submarine.

SS-N-9

Status:	In service on Charlie II and possibly on Papa class.
Dimensions:	Length, 30ft (9.1m); diameter, not known; wingspan, not known.
Launch weight:	Not known.
Propulsion:	Single-stage solid fuel motor.
Guidance:	Active radar homing.
Range:	60+ miles (96km).
Flight speed:	Mach 0.9.
Warhead:	HE or nuclear.

It is known that SS-N-9 is deployed on Nanuchka class missile patrol boats. It is also mounted on Charlie II class SSGNs and may be carried by the single Papa class boat as well. Few details are known in the West and the specifications above are provisional. It is of interest that the Nanuchka class warships exported to India are armed with SS-N-2 or SS-N-11 missiles and not with SS-N-9, which is carried by all Soviet Navy Nanuchka missile patrol boats.

Subroc

Status:	First deployed 1965 on Permit class SSNs; now also in service on Sturgeon and Los Angeles class. Production ended 1978.
Dimensions:	Length, 20ft 6in (6.25m); diameter, 21in (53cm).
Launch weight:	4,085lb (1,853kg).
Propulsion:	Thiokol TE-260G solid motor.
Guidance:	SD-510 inertial system by Kearfott division of Singer-General Precision.
Range:	Maximum 35 miles (56.3km).
Flight speed:	Supersonic.
Warhead:	Nuclear depth bomb with 3 to 5 mile (5 to 8km) lethal radius.

The UUM-44A Subroc (Submarine Rocket) is a unique weapon system which is launched from a submerged submarine, leaves the water, travels at supersonic speed through the air, and then deposits its warhead into the water again to attack another submerged submarine. It was conceived in 1955 and development began in 1958, but, not surprisingly, the project was dogged by very severe problems. Persistence had its reward, however, and it reached IOC in 1965.

Subroc is fired from a standard 21in (533mm) torpedo tube. Its guidance system is activated and updated by the submarine's attack systems prior to launch, and on leaving the tube it begins to follow a programmed mission profile. Within one second of tube exit, the solid-fuel motor ignites and the missile heads for the surface, leaving the water at an exit angle of about 30°. It then accelerates to supersonic speed, until the guidance system cuts off the motor and explosive bolts detach the warhead. The warhead is guided by an inertial system using reverse-thrust rockets to slow it down and small aerodynamic control surfaces. Water re-entry is achieved while at supersonic speed, whereupon the device sinks to the required depth before detonation.

Production ended in 1978 and a successor—currently known as the 'ASW Stand-off Weapon'—is being developed by Boeing in co-operation with Gould Ocean Systems Division, with an anticipated IOC of 1986. Range is estimated as 68 to 100 miles (110 to 160km).

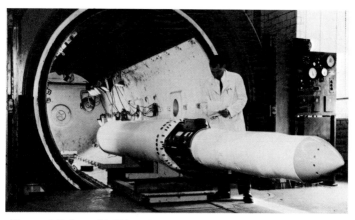

Above: A Subroc SLCM on hydrostatic pressure test at the Naval Ordnance Laboratory, White Oak, Maryland, in October 1964.

Above: Fired from the standard 21in (533mm) torpedo tube of a submerged SSN, Subroc breaks surface at a typical launch angle.

Nuclear-Powered Attack Submarines

The first American nuclear-powered submarine was completed in 1954 after an almost unparalleled development effort, giving the USA an estimated five-year lead over the USSR. The Soviet Navy has now overtaken the US Navy in terms of numbers of SSNs, but few of the Soviet nuclear-powered attack submarines possess the advanced features common to all American boats since the early 1960s. The British and French navies are the only others with SSNs, although there are unconfirmed reports that the Chinese have one SSN on trials.

United States of America

The earliest SSNs still in front-line service with the US Navy are the five Skipjacks, small, handy boats capable of speeds well over 30 knots. They lack the advanced sonar systems, however, and are conventionally armed with six bow torpedo tubes. The Permit and Sturgeon classes which followed are larger, carry a more advanced sonar outfit, and fire Subroc, a nuclear-tipped anti-submarine missile with a range of 28-34 miles (46-56km). As there was no increase in output power, speed in these classes fell to 28 knots.

The current type, still under construction, is the Los Angeles class, which shows a 50 per cent increase in displacement over earlier SSNs. In addition to the installation of more advanced sensors and fire control equipment (now being retrofitted in the Permit and Sturgeon boats) the Los Angeles class has regained the speed lost since the Skipjacks.

Operating procedures in the Soviet Navy make it unlikely that there would be task groups of surface ships against which American SSNs could be concentrated, although with the advent of Kiev class carriers and Kirov class battlecruisers the Soviets seem to be generating such targets! American SSNs are, therefore, designed for three basic roles: ASW hunter-killer; independent forward area attack and reconnaissance; and the protection of task groups and convoys. The key to success in operations against other submarines is quietness, which enables the hunter to avoid detection, allied to a powerful suite of sensors with which to detect an opponent at the earliest possible moment. Whereas SSNs of other navies have their torpedo tubes in the bow, US Navy submarines since the Permit class have had their tubes amidships, freeing the bow for a large active sonar with passive hydrophones along the outside of the hull. This is not only the most favourable position for detection, but also keeps the sensors away from the propulsion unit.

Nuclear propulsion is a relatively noisy way of powering a submarine, particularly at the high speeds which constitute its main advantage over diesel-electric plant, but successive designs have shown a steady improvement in this respect. In the Los Angeles boats particular attention has been paid to quiet operation, the large hull making it easier to 'cushion' the machinery. The increase in speed in the Los Angeles class also reflects an increasing tactical requirement for the defence of fast carrier task groups against Soviet SSGNs. All American SSNs except the Skipjacks will be fitted with Harpoon missiles in the near future, giving them a new capability against surface units. Harpoon, unlike Soviet cruise missiles, does not need a purpose-built submarine to launch it, being purpose-designed to fit a 21in (533mm) torpedo tube. The great majority of American SSNs are based in the Atlantic, where they would play a crucial part in a future war by keeping open the essential sea-lanes to Europe.

Above: USS *Guardfish* (SSN-612) of the Permit (Thresher) class has four 21in (533mm) torpedo tubes amidships. These boats fire the Subroc A/S missile and will soon carry Harpoon.

United Kingdom

The other SSNs in NATO are those of the British and French navies. The earliest of the British boats, HMS *Dreadnought,* has an American Skipjack propulsion unit, but the later Valiant, Swiftsure and Trafalgar classes are of completely British design.

The British boats have generally followed the pattern of development of their US Navy counter-parts. The Valiant class corre-sponds roughly with the Permit, and the Swiftsure with the Stur-geon. Frequent deployments take place in company with surface units, and the designation Fleet

Submarine makes it clear that the British see the role of their SSNs in the same light as the Americans. Interestingly, however, the Royal Navy boats always have torpedo tubes in the bow and there is no equivalent to Subroc, although Harpoon will soon be fitted.

France

Other navies have progressed from SSN to SSBN, but France was forced for political and economic reasons to do it the other way round. Top defence priority was given to the SSBN force and until this programme was virtually com-plete no resources or finance could

be spared for SSNs. The first French SSN *(Rubis)* was not, therefore, laid down until 1976 and did not join the fleet until 1982. She will be joined by three more sisters in a fairly slow building programme over the next five to six years. These are the smallest operational SSNs yet built—2,670 tons submerged—and there will be one squadron in the Atlantic and a second in the Mediterranean.

Soviet Union

The fifteen November class submarines were the first nuclear-powered boats to be built for the Soviet Navy and were based on the products of an intelligence operation rather than on lengthy national research. They are much longer than contemporary American SSNs, their hull casing is lined with free-flood holes, and they have an extremely noisy propulsion unit, which, nevertheless, drives them at a maximum submerged speed of 30 knots. Following the abandonment of their original strategic mission, for which they were armed with a nuclear-tipped torpedo, the Novembers were given an anti-carrier role, using conventional torpedoes. Their value even in this role is now questionable, given the capability of modern sensors and ASW aircraft.

The other major class of SSNs in Soviet service is the Victor class, the first of which appeared in 1968, and which has continued in production, albeit with some modifications, into the 1980s. A second-generation SSN, it has an improved hull form, greater diving depth, a much quieter propulsion system, and a submerged speed of about 30 knots. Later versions of the Victor are thought to be armed with the SS-N-15.

The Soviet SSN fleet has been boosted by the conversion of missile-carrying types which were no longer required in that role.

Above: British Valiant class fleet submarine *Conqueror* (S-48) in 1981, armed only with conventional torpedoes.

Above left: USS *Nautilus* (SSN-571), seen in 1965, was the first nuclear-propelled submarine, making her first voyage in 1955.

Left: Soviet Victor I SSN has six 21in (533mm) bow torpedo tubes. Victor II and III may carry the SS-N-15 A/S missile.

Thus, five Echo I SSGNs and five Yankee class SSBNs are now all SSNs, a useful addition in terms of numbers, although they are probably not as efficient as those boats purpose-designed for the role.

The Northern Fleet has been allocated nearly all the modern Victors, together with about half the older Novembers. The Pacific Fleet thus has the remaining Novembers, the five Echo Is and a few Victors.

Outside the general run of Soviet SSN development are the Alfa class submarines. These are very small for nuclear boats, indicating an advanced reactor design, and the use of titanium in their construction is thought to give them a diving depth of some 3,000 ft (914m). They are credited with the astonishing underwater speed of 42 knots, which, even given their small size, would be a remarkable technical achievement. Problems with leaks in the hull casing, however, appear to have caused long delays in putting this class into full production and the prototype was broken up. The Alfa was almost certainly conceived for the anti-SSBN mission, although it is difficult to see how it would locate its target, particularly in the open ocean. The combination of high speed and great diving depth would make the Alfa itself difficult to hit, even if it could be detected in the first place. US concern on this point is evidenced by experiments recently initiated with a new deep-diving homing torpedo.

China

Unconfirmed reports credit the Chinese Navy with the construction of at least two SSNs of the 'Han' class. These would doubtless have an Albacore type hull. China certainly has the technical ability to produce an SSN, but hard evidence of the existence of these boats has yet to be established.

Nautilus Class/Skate Class

Total built: Nautilus: 1; Skate: 4.
Launched: Nautilus: 21 January 1954; Skate: 1957-58.
Status: Nautilus: national museum; Skate: 4 in service.
Displacement: Nautilus: 3,674 tons (surfaced), 4,040 tons (submerged);
Skate: 2,360 tons (surfaced), 2,547 tons (submerged).
Dimensions: Nautilus: length, 319ft 5in (97.4m); beam, 27ft 7in (8.4m); draught, 22ft (6.7m).
Skate: length, 267ft 8in (81.6m); beam, 25ft (7.6m); draught, 22ft (6.7m).
Torpedo tubes: Nautilus: six 21in (533mm);
Skate: eight 21in (533mm).
Propulsion: Nautilus: nuclear (15,000shp);
Skate: nuclear (6,600shp).
Shafts: Nautilus/Skate: two.
Speed: Nautilus: 20+kt, 37km/hr (surfaced), 20kt, 37km/hr (submerged);
Skate: 20+kt, 37km/hr (surfaced), 25+kt, 46km/hr (submerged).
Complement: Nautilus: 105; Skate: 87.

Not many ships can be positively identified as true turning-points in maritime history. The first all-big-gun battleship, HMS *Dreadnought,* was such a turning-point; so, too, was USS *Nautilus.* The first ever nuclear-propelled submarine, *Nautilus* showed how the navies of the future could become truly independent of the surface, patrolling the depths of the oceans, their endurance limited only by the physical and mental qualities of their crews.

The first funds for the construction of a nuclear submarine were authorised by Congress in the FY52 budget, following research and development on a submarine reactor begun by the Argonne National Laboratory in 1948 and continued by Westinghouse. The resultant Submarine Thermal Reactor Mark II, designated the S2W, was installed in the hull of *Nautilus* during her 27-month construction. On 17 January 1955, she was able to signal 'Under way on nuclear power', giving the USA a three to four year lead on the USSR.

Below: On 17 March 1959, USS *Skate* (SSN-578) made the first surfacing by a submarine at the North Pole. *Skate* surfaced, as seen here, ten times in all during this polar cruise.

Below right: USS *Nautilus* (SSN-571), the first-ever nuclear propelled submarine, first got under way on 17 January 1955.

Nautilus was designed with a conventional streamlined hull which, nevertheless, allowed a maximum speed well in excess of 20 knots. By August 1958 she had established sufficient confidence to be sent on the first submarine polar transit, starting from Hawaii and finishing at Portland, England. *Nautilus* steamed 62,562 miles (100,681km) on her first nuclear core; 91,324 miles (146,968km) on her second; and some 150,000 miles (241,935km) on her third. When she goes on public display in the USA, the historic reactor will remain on board (defuelled and in a safe state) and a token crew of two officers and twentyfour enlisted men will be responsible for keeping house aboard this unique and truly historic boat.

By 1958 two other nuclear boats were at sea: *Seawolf*, with an unsuccessful S2G liquid-sodium-cooled reactor (she now has a pressurised-water plant similar to that in *Nautilus* and is used for research work); and the first of the four Skate class. The Skates were the first production nuclear boats, similar in general layout to *Nautilus* but somewhat smaller. Like *Nautilus* they established many submarine 'firsts', including the first-ever surfacing at the North Pole (USS *Skate* on 17 March 1959). All four boats, after a number of refits and refuellings, remain operational with the Pacific Fleet.

Two more nuclear submarines were built at the same time as the Skates: the Regulus I armed *Halibut* and the radar picket *Triton*. Both were optimised for surface operation, and for a variety of reasons were less than successful. They were used for a period as SSNs, but are now in reserve; whether they could ever be returned to active duty must now be somewhat questionable.

Below: *Nautilus*, seen here on trials, decommissioned in March 1980 and is to be preserved at Washington Navy Yard.

Skipjack Class

Total built:	Six.
Launched:	1958-60.
Status:	Five in service.
Displacement:	3,075 tons (surfaced); 3,513 tons (submerged).
Dimensions:	Length, 251ft 8in (76.6m); beam, 31ft 6in (9.6m); draught, 29ft 5in (8.9m).
Torpedo tubes:	Six 21in (533mm).
Propulsion:	Nuclear (15,000shp).
Speed:	16+kt, 30km/hr (surfaced); 30+kt, 55.5km/hr (submerged).
Complement:	93.

The Skipjack class SSNs were the first nuclear submarines to incorporate the teardrop hull developed in the conventionally-powered USS *Albacore* (AGSS-569). Hence, whereas her predecessors had a submerged speed of some 20+ knots, USS *Skipjack*, with her new hull form, is capable of well over 30 knots, although her surface performance is poor in comparison. As well as the improved speed, underwater manoeuvrability is also increased, although the use of only one screw brings its own problems and means that stern torpedo tubes can no longer be fitted.

One of this class, *Scorpion* (SSN-589), was modified on the slip to become the first of the George Washington class SSBNs, and the materials for another of the Skipjack class were appropriated for USS *Patrick Henry*. Ultimately, six Skipjacks were built between 1956 and 1961, including a replacement for *Scorpion* (SSN-589) which had been lost with all hands in the Atlantic in May 1968.

All engine fittings in the Skipjacks (except for the reactor and the propeller) are duplicated to minimise the danger of a breakdown. They have had their original sonar equipment updated, but these old boats will not be fitted with the BQQ-5 sonar because they have their torpedo tubes in the old bow position. They were the first boats to use the S5W nuclear reactor, but they are now reaching the termination of their active lives.

Above right: USS *Skipjack's* surfaced speed (16+ kt) is poor in comparison to a submerged 30+ kt with a 'tear-drop' hull.

Right: The underwater manoeuvrability of the nuclear-powered *Skipjack* (SSN-585) is improved by fin-mounted diving planes.

Below: Significant for advanced design in 1958-60, the Skipjack SSNs are now reaching the end of their operational careers.

Sturgeon Class/Narwhal Class

Total built:	Sturgeon: 37; Narwhal: 1.
Launched:	Sturgeon: 1966-74; Narwhal: 1967.
Status:	Sturgeon: 37 in service; Narwhal: 1 in service.
Displacement:	Sturgeon: 3,640 tons (surfaced), 4,640 tons (submerged); Narwhal: 4,450 tons (surfaced), 5,350 tons (submerged).
Dimensions:	Sturgeon: length, 292ft 2in (89m); beam, 31ft 8in (9.7m); draught, 26ft (7.9m). Narwhal: length, 314ft 7in (95.9m); beam, 37ft 8in (11.5m); draught, 27ft (8.2m).
Torpedo tubes:	Sturgeon/Narwhal: four 21in (533mm) amidships.
A/S weapons:	Sturgeon/Narwhal: Subroc; A/S torpedoes.
Propulsion:	Sturgeon: nuclear (15,000shp); Narwhal: nuclear (17,000shp).
Speed:	Sturgeon/Narwhal: 20+kt, 37km/hr (surfaced); 30+kt, 55.5km/hr (submerged).
Complement:	Sturgeon/Narwhal: 107.

The 37 Sturgeon class SSNs are slightly enlarged and improved versions of the Permit (Thresher) class. Like them, the Sturgeons have an elongated teardrop hull with torpedo tubes set amidships, with the bow taken up by the various components of the BQQ-2 sonar system. The Sturgeon is distinguished visually from the Permit by its taller fin with the driving planes set farther down. Several problems arose between the USN and the builders of this class: *Pogy* (SSN-647) was re-allocated to another yard for completion, while *Guitarro* (SSN-665) was delayed for more than two years after sinking in 35ft (10.7m) of water while being fitted out, in an incident later described by a Congressional committee as 'wholly avoidable'.

Above: USS *Narwhal* (SSN-671), built to test the S5G free-circulation reactor, remains in service as the only USN submarine with this system.

Right: A Sturgeon class SSN. The tall sail rises to a height of 20ft 6in (6.25m) above the submarine's deck.

In an attempt to reduce noise, the Sturgeon class is fitted with two contra-rotating propellers on the same shaft. Although American submarines are already significantly quieter than their Soviet counterparts, any developments which can reduce noise (and therefore the distance at which the submarine can be detected) are speedily introduced. The Sturgeons, like the Permits, will be fitted during the course of routine overhauls with the BQQ-5 sonar system introduced in the Los Angeles class.

Narwhal (SSN-671), an experimental SSN based on the Permit/Sturgeon design, was built in 1967-69 to test the S5G free-circulation reactor, which has no pumps and is therefore quieter than previous US reactors. Although *Narwhal* retains this sytem and is still in service, no further submarines have been built with such a system.

Above: A Mark 48 Mod 1 torpedo aboard USS *Pargo* (SSN-650). Sturgeon class SSNs mount four 21in (533mm) tubes amidships.

Below: Sturgeon class submarines like *Sea Devil* (SSN-664), here seen surfacing, have a diving depth of 1,320ft (400m).

Tullibee Class/ Permit (Thresher) Class

Total built:	Tullibee: 1; Permit: 14.
Launched:	Tullibee: 1960; Permit: 1961-66.
Status:	Tullibee: 1 in service; Permit: 13 in service.
Displacement:	Tullibee: 2,317 tons (surfaced), 2,640 tons (submerged);
	Permit: 3,750 tons (surfaced), 4,300 tons (submerged).
Dimensions:	Tullibee: length, 273ft (83.2m); beam, 23ft 4in (7.1m); draught, 21ft (6.4m).
	Permit: length, 278ft 6in (84.9m); beam, 31ft 8in (9.6m); draught, 28ft 5in (8.7m).
Missiles:	Tullibee: nil; Permit: Sub-Harpoon.
Torpedo tubes:	Tullibee/Permit: four 21in (533mm).
A/S weapons:	Tullibee: A/S torpedoes;
	Permit: A/S torpedoes, Subroc.
Propulsion:	Tullibee: nuclear (2,500shp);
	Permit: nuclear (15,000shp).
Shafts:	Tullibee/Permit: one.
Speed:	Tullibee: 15+kt, 28km/hr (surfaced), 20+kt, 37km/hr (submerged);
	Permit: 20+kt, 37km/hr (surfaced), 30+kt, 55.5km/hr (submerged).
Complement:	Tullibee: 56; Permit: 103.

Tullibee is one of the smallest SSNs to be built, displacing only 2,640 tons submerged, and was an early attempt at the ideal hunter-killer submarine. The small size meant that she was very manoeuvrable and thus more likely to detect a hostile submarine before herself being detected. The torpedo tubes were fitted amidships for the first time in order to free the bows for the then new BQQ-2 conformal sonar array. She was also fitted with turbo-electric drive to eliminate the noise made by the reduction gears in earlier boats. However, small size also led to a low submerged speed, and *Tullibee* lacked space to carry the more sophisticated (and inevitably larger) equipment and electronics. No more SSNs of this size have been built for the US Navy. *Tullibee* remains in service but is no longer considered a first-line unit.

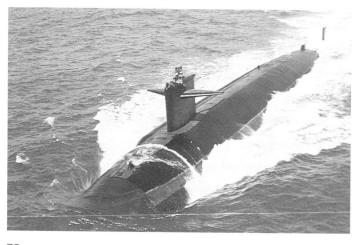

All the better features of *Tullibee* were incorporated into the Thresher class, which, after the loss of the name ship in the Atlantic in April 1963, was redesignated the Permit class. Built between 1960 and 1966, four of these boats were originally designed to take the Regulus II cruise missile: they were re-ordered as SSNs when the Regulus II was cancelled in favour of the Polaris SLBM in 1958. The last three of the class (SSN-614, -615 and -621) have a larger hull than the earlier boats; *Jack* (SSN-605) has a modified hull to accommodate contra-rotating propellers, as one of the US Navy's many attempts to find a really quiet propulsion system. The principal anti-submarine weapon is Subroc, controlled by the BQQ-2 sonar sytem; the Permits can also fire the anti-ship Harpoon missile. They will in time be fitted to take the Tomahawk SLCM and will also be retrofitted with the BQQ-5 sonar.

Below left: SSN of the Permit class; first designated Thresher class but changed after the loss of the name ship in 1963.

Below: USS *Barb* (SSN-596) of the Permit class. This class was the first to carry Subroc guided by the BQQ-2 sonar system.

Bottom: Experimental hunter-killer *Tullibee* (SSN-597); small, manoeuvrable but lacking equipment space and submerged speed.

Lipscomb Class/ Los Angeles Class

Total built:	Lipscomb: 1; Los Angeles: 19 (+ 18).
Launched:	Lipscomb: 1973; Los Angeles: 1974-83.
Status:	Lipscomb: 1 in service;
	Los Angeles: 19 in service, 11 building, 7 ordered.
Dimensions:	Lipscomb: length, 365ft (111.3m); beam, 31ft 8in (9.7m); draught, 31ft (9.5m).
	Los Angeles: length, 360ft (109.7m); beam, 33ft (10.1m); draught, 32ft 4in (9.8m).
Missiles:	Lipscomb: Harpoon;
	Los Angeles: Harpoon, Tomahawk.
Torpedo tubes:	Lipscomb/Los Angeles: four 21in (533mm) (amidships).
A/S weapons:	Lipscomb: Subroc;
	Los Angeles: Subroc, Mk 48 torpedoes.
Propulsion:	Lipscomb: nuclear;
	Los Angeles: nuclear (35,000shp).
Shafts:	Lipscomb/Los Angeles: one.
Speed:	Lipscomb: 25+kt, 46km/hr (submerged);
	Los Angeles: 30+kt, 55.5km/hr (submerged).
Complement:	Lipscomb: 120; Los Angeles: 127.

USS *Glenard P. Lipscomb* was launched in 1973, the outcome of a development programme for a 'quiet' submarine stretching back to USS *Tullibee* of the early 1960s. *Lipscomb* has many interesting features to achieve silent running, many of them subsequently incorporated into the Los Angeles class. Like *Tullibee, Lipscomb* is powered by a pressurised-water cooled reactor driving a turbo-electric plant. This removes the requirement for gearing, which is one of the prime sources of noise in submarines. Although *Lipscomb* remains in front-line service, this particular drive system was not repeated in the submarines of the Los Angeles class.

Right: Banner is removed from bow of Los Angeles class USS *Dallas* (SSN-700) after launching ceremony, 28 April 1979.

Below: USS *Philadelphia* (SSN-690): the unit cost of each Los Angeles, the largest SSNs built, rose to $495.8 million in 1981.

The first Los Angeles SSN entered service in 1976; nineteen are now in commission, eleven are under construction and a further seven are on order. They are much larger than any previous SSN and have a higher submerged speed. They have the BQQ-5 sonar system and can operate Subroc, Sub-Harpoon and Tomahawk as well as conventional and wire-guided torpedoes. Thus, like all later US SSNs, although they are intended to hunt other submarines and to protect SSBNs they can also be used without modification to sink surface ships at long range with Sub-Harpoon. Further, Tomahawk will enable them to operate against strategic targets well inland.

The Los Angeles class is very sophisticated and each boat is an extremely potent fighting machine. With a production run of at least 37, it must be considered a very successful design. However, these boats are becoming very expensive: in 1976 the cost of each one was estimated at $221.25 million; the boat bought in 1979 cost $325.6 million; the two in 1981 will cost $495.8 million each. Not even the USA can continue to spend money at that rate.

Nevertheless, the Reagan Administration has ordered a speeding up of the Los Angeles building programme, calling for two in 1982 and three per year thereafter. The Tomahawk missile programme is also being accelerated: Tomahawk will be fitted from SSN-719 (the twenty-second boat to be launched, in 1983) onward.

A design for a smaller and cheaper SSN, under consideration in 1980 as a result of Congressional pressure, appears to have been shelved. There are now plans to improve the Los Angeles boats—especially their sensors, weapon systems and control equipment—and consideration is also being given to a vertically-launched cruise missile system which would comprise 12 vertical tubes, possibly mounted in the forward main ballast tank area.

Right: *Philadelphia* **on immediate pre-commissioning trials, 1977.**

Below: Los Angeles class *Baton Rouge* **(SSN-689) at sea, 1977.**

George Washington Class/ Ethan Allen Class

Total built: Washington: 5; Allen: 5.
Launched: Washington: 1959-60; Allen: 1960-62.
Converted: Washington: 1981-82; Allen: 1981-84.
Status: Washington: three under conversion, two laid up; Allen: all under conversion.
Displacement: Washington: 6,019 tons (surfaced), 6,888 tons (submerged); Allen: 6,955 tons (surfaced), 7,880 tons (submerged).
Dimensions: Washington: length, 381ft 8in (116.3m); beam, 33ft (10.1m); draught, 29ft (8.8m). Allen: length, 410ft (125m); beam, 33ft (10.1m); draught, 32ft (9.8m).
Torpedo tubes: Washington: six 21in (533mm); Allen: four 21in (533mm).
Propulsion: Washington/Allen: nuclear (15,000shp).
Shafts: Washington/Allen: one.
Speed: Washington: 20kt, 37km/hr (surfaced), 31kt, 57km/hr (submerged); Allen: 20kt, 37km/hr (surfaced), 30kt, 55.5km/hr (submerged).
Complement: Washington: 112, Allen: 142.

Inset below: USS *George Washington* (SSBN-598),currently converting to SSN, is seen here under way on trials in 1959.

The George Washington class, like the German Type XXI and USS *Nautilus,* have their place in history as the first nuclear-powered ballistic missile armed submarines, a concept which changed the strategic picture radically in the 1960s. In order to bring the Polaris SLBM into service as soon as possible, the five George Washington SSBNs were basically lengthened versions of the Skipjack class SSNs. In fact, *George Washington* (SSBN-598) herself was laid down as *Scorpion* (SSN-589), and was lengthened by the addition of a 130ft (40m) insert while on the stocks. The original powerplant and much of the SSN-type equipment was retained in the SSBN. The five George Washington SSBNs were in service for seven years before the first of the Soviet equivalents, the Yankee class, became operational. By the mid-1960s the relatively short range of the Polaris A-1 missiles was making the George Washingtons vulnerable to Soviet countermeasures, so during their first re-coring they were fitted with the 2,855-mile (4,595km) Polaris A-3. Their electronics were also upgraded.

Two of this class (*Theodore Roosevelt* and *Abraham Lincoln*) had their missile compartments removed in 1980 and the spent fuel disposed of. Although the bow and stern sections were then rejoined, the decommissioned hulks are now being cannibalized for spares prior to disposal. The three remaining boats are being converted to SSNs by removing all missiles and associated equipment; cement will be put into the missile tubes as ballast compensation. The cost of conversion is a mere $400,000 per boat. As SSNs, their main use will be in training and as targets on ASW exercises, thus releasing more modern SSNs for front-line duties. The three boats will only be used in this way for two to three years, however, because of the short life remaining in their nuclear cores.

Below: *Thomas A. Edison,* 1971. The five Ethan Allens, USN's first specially designed SSBNs, are to be converted to SSNs.

Whereas the George Washington class was built to a modified SSN design in order to get the Polaris into service as soon as possible, the five Ethan Allen SSBNs were the first to be specially designed as such. While generally similar to the George Washingtons, they are nearly 30ft (9.1m) longer and, when first commissioned, were armed with the Polaris A-2, which had a range of 1,725 miles (2,776km). They had greatly improved crew quarters, an important factor in boats which remained submerged for more than sixty days at a time. *Ethan Allen* herself became the first SSBN to fire a live SLBM, on 6 May 1962; this detonated successfully on the Christmas Island test range. These boats were fitted with Polaris A-3, but, like the George Washingtons, they will not be fitted with Poseidon or Trident. All five are now being converted to SSNs and will operate in the attack role through to the end of the 1980s at least.

Right: Ethan Allen class *Thomas Jefferson* will undergo SSN conversion in FY1984, with missiles and associated equipment removed and missile tubes packed with cement as ballast.

Below: Seen as an SSBN in January 1978, this Ethan Allen class was then armed with sixteen tubes for the Polaris A-3 SLBM. These boats will serve as SSNs throughout the 1980s.

November Class

Total built:	Fifteen.
Launched:	1957-62.
Status:	Thirteen in service; one in reserve.
Displacement:	4,200 tons (surfaced); 5,000 tons (submerged).
Dimensions:	Length, 359ft 10in (109.7m); beam, 29ft 10in (9.1m); draught, 21ft 11in (6.7m).
Torpedo tubes:	Eight 21in (533mm) (bow); two 16in (406mm) (stern).
Propulsion:	Nuclear (30,000shp).
Shafts:	Two.
Speed:	30kt, 55.5km/hr (submerged).
Complement:	86.

These large and generally conservatively designed boats were the first Soviet submarines to have nuclear propulsion. To a great degree the technology was based upon intelligence information gained from the United States in 1955, although at the time the USSR failed to appreciate the advantages of the 'tear-drop' hull first seen in the US Navy's *Albacore*. Accordingly, Soviet designers gave the Novembers a long conventional hull with two screws. By 1963 a total of 15 had been commissioned, despite the fact that they had long since been overtaken by later technology, illustrating the inflexibility of Soviet construction programmes, allied to their preference for long production runs.

One November class submarine sank in the Atlantic southwest of the UK in April 1970. Most, if not all, of the crew were saved. No nuclear contamination has been detected in the area.

Below: A Soviet November class SSN surfaced and in difficulty in the Atlantic Ocean, where a boat of this class sank, southwest of the United Kingdom, in April 1970.

November class SSN.

Top: The Novembers were the first Soviet nuclear-propelled submarines. The many free-flood holes in the casing must give rise to considerable noise.

Above: A Soviet merchant ship stands by to aid a November class SSN which appears to have surfaced in distress.

Victor Class

Total built:	Victor I: 16; Victor II: 6; Victor III: 11(+?).
Launched:	Victor I: 1966-68; Victor II: 1971-78; Victor III: 1976-?
Status:	Victor I: 16 in service; Victor II: 7 in service; Victor III: 5 in service.
Displacement:	Victor I: 4,300 tons (surfaced, 5,300 tons (submerged); Victor II: 4,700 tons (surfaced), 5,680 tons (submerged); Victor III: 5,000 tons (surfaced), 6,000 tons (submerged).
Dimensions:	Victor I: length, 307ft 8in (93.8m); beam, 32ft 10in (10m); draught, 23ft 11in (7.3m). Victor II: length, 328ft 1in (100m); beam, 32ft 10in (10m); draught, 23ft 11in (7.3m). Victor III: length, 337ft 11in (103m); beam, 32ft 10in (10m); draught, 23ft 11in (7.3m).
Missiles:	Victor I: SS-N-15; Victor II: SS-N-15; Victor III: SS-N-15/SS-NX-16.
Torpedo tubes:	Victor I/II/III: six 21in (533mm).
Propulsion:	Victor I/II/III: nuclear (30,000shp).
Shafts:	Victor I/II/III: one main; two quiet.
Speed:	Victor I: 32kt, 59km/hr (submerged); Victor II: 31kt, 57km/hr (submerged); Victor III: 30kt, 55.5km/hr (submerged).
Complement:	Victor I: 100; Victor II: 110; Victor III: 120.

First seen by Western observers in 1968, the Victor class is a second-generation Soviet nuclear-powered attack submarine. Somewhat shorter than the November boats, but with as great a beam, sixteen of the first type—Victor I—were built. These were followed by the Victor II, which is 15.4ft (4.7m) longer and is generally assumed to be capable of carrying the SS-N-15 missile. Only six of these boats were built before production shifted to yet another development, Victor III, which is still longer and has an interesting cylindrical object mounted on top of the upper rudder, possibly some form of towed sonar array. A Park Lamp direction finder antenna has been identified as standard on Victors.

Top: Soviet nuclear-powered attack submarine of Victor class on patrol in the South China Sea. Twentyeight boats of Victor I, II and III types are currently in Soviet Navy service.

Above: As is suggested in this picture, Victor class SSNs were the first Soviet boats with an Albacore-style hull form.

Below left: The Victor II SSN is some 15ft (4.5m) longer than Victor I; probably to accommodate the SS-N-15 missile.

Below right: Shadow of the shadower—a US Navy aircraft makes a low run over a surfaced Victor class SSN, April 1974.

Alfa Class

Total built:	Five +.
Launched:	1970-?
Status:	Three in service.
Displacement:	3,500 tons (surfaced); 4,200 tons (submerged).
Dimensions:	Length, 260ft 1in (79.3m); beam, 32ft 10in (10.0m); draught, 24ft 11in (7.6m).
Torpedo tubes:	Six 21in (533mm).
Propulsion:	Nuclear (24,000shp).
Shafts:	One.
Speed:	40+kt, 74km/hr (submerged).
Complement:	60.

The first Alfa class SSN was completed at the Sudomekh yard in Leningrad in 1970 and, after protracted tests, was scrapped in 1974. Either this boat was deliberately built as a prototype, as is done in the case of aircraft, or it was found to be a failure in some material respect. The second of the class was laid down in 1971, the third in 1976 and the fourth in 1977: production continues at a very slow rate.

The Alfa class boats are very much shorter than previous Soviet SSNs, indicating the possibility of a new and much smaller nuclear reactor. They certainly are capable of very great speeds and have been reported as having run under NATO task forces on exercise at such speeds that effective action against them in a combat environment would have been virtually impossible. The hull is reported to be constructed of titanium alloy, conferring a maximum diving depth of some 3,000ft (914m). Indeed, the long construction time may be related to difficult fabrication to achieve such remarkable strength, and the use of new materials. The long, low fin and the total absence of any protruding devices in published photographs is also of interest.

It would appear that the Soviet Navy has come up with something unusual in the Alfa class: it is a type that needs to be examined with great care by Western defence authorities.

Above: Note the long, low fin, with no protruding devices (other than retractable aerials) of this Alfa class SSN.

Bottom: Alfa class SSN under way. A hull of titanium alloy permits these submarines to dive to some 3,000ft (914m).

Alfa class SSN.

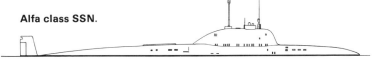

Dreadnought Class/ Valiant Class

Total built:	Dreadnought: 1; Valiant: 5.
Launched:	Dreadnought: 1960; Valiant: 1963-70.
Status:	Dreadnought: 0 in service; Valiant: 5 in service.
Displacement:	Dreadnought: 3,500 tons (surfaced), 4,000 tons (submerged); Valiant: 4,400 tons (surfaced), 4,900 tons (submerged).
Dimensions:	Dreadnought: length, 265ft 10in (81m); beam, 32ft 2in (9.8m); draught, 26ft (7.9m). Valiant: length, 285ft (86.9m); beam, 33ft 2in (10.1m); draught, 27ft (8.2m).
Torpedo tubes:	Dreadnought/Valiant: six 21in (533mm).
Propulsion:	Dreadnought/Valiant: nuclear (15,000shp).
Shafts:	Dreadnought/Valiant: one.
Speed:	Dreadnought: 15kt, 28km/hr (surfaced), 25kt, 46km/hr (submerged); Valiant: 15kt, 28km/hr (surfaced), 28kt, 52km/hr (submerged).
Complement:	Dreadnought: 88; Valiant: 103.

Britain studied the possibilities of nuclear-powered submarines from 1946. In 1954 a naval section was set up at the Atomic Research Station, Harwell, and cooperated with the Admiralty, Vickers-Armstrong, Rolls-Royce and Foster-Wheeler to design a land-based prototype submarine reactor, built at Dounreay from spring 1958. It was based on the American Westinghouse S5W pressurised water-cooled reactor and first went critical in 1965.

Above: HMS *Churchill,* an SSN of the Valiant class, the first
entirely British nuclear fleet submarines, is seen here
at the Faslane base of 3rd Squadron, Submarine Command.

Below: Commissioned in 1963, Britain's first nuclear submarine
—powered by an American S5W reactor—was HMS *Dreadnought,*
here seen at speed on the surface, April 1974, en route to a refit.

To speed up the British nuclear submarine programme, a complete S5W reactor was bought from the USA and used to power the first British nuclear boat, HMS *Dreadnought*. The bow section of this boat, containing the Type 2001 sonar, was of wholly British design and is much blunter than USS *Skipjack's*. Unlike later American SSNs, all British nuclear submarines have the foreplanes mounted on the bow rather than on the fin.

Because *Dreadnought* is much deeper diving than previous British submarines, her hull was carefully checked for cracks and much time was spent in repairing them during the first years that she was in commission. She also underwent a major overhaul from May 1968 to September 1970, when the reactor core was renewed.

Above: Note the absence of fin-mounted foreplanes on HMS *Dreadnought*; unlike the later American SSNs, all British nuclear submarines have foreplanes mounted on the bow.

Below: Crew member at his station aboard HMS *Valiant* (S-102).

The first entirely British nuclear submarine, *Valiant,* was ordered in August 1960 and completed in July 1966. Although 19ft (5.8m) longer than *Dreadnought* and with a somewhat larger complement, the Valiant class is otherwise generally similar. Four more Valiants were built before production switched to the Swiftsure class.

In 1967, HMS *Valiant* travelled 10,000 miles (16,093km) submerged from Singapore to the UK in 28 days. *Dreadnought* was taken out of service in 1981, and in February 1982 it was announced that she would be scrapped. The Valiants will serve on well into the 1990s.

Below: A Valiant SSN runs semi-submerged. In 1967, HMS *Valiant* completed a 10,000-mile (16,093km), 28-day voyage submerged.

Swiftsure Class/Trafalgar Class

Total built: Swiftsure: 6; Trafalgar 1 (+3).
Launched: Swiftsure: 1971-79; Trafalgar: 1981-84.
Status: Swiftsure: 6 in service; Trafalgar: 1 fitting out.
Displacement: Swiftsure: 4,200 tons (surfaced), 4,500 tons (submerged); Trafalgar: not known.
Dimensions: Swiftsure: length, 272ft (82.9m); beam, 32ft 4in (9.8m); draught, 27ft (8.2m).
Trafalgar: not known.
Torpedo tubes: Swiftsure: five 21in (533mm).
Propulsion: Swiftsure: nuclear (15,000shp); auxiliary diesel (4,000hp).
Shafts: Swiftsure/Trafalgar: one.
Speed: Swiftsure: 30kt, 55.5km/hr (submerged).
Complement: Swiftsure: 97; Trafalgar: not known.

The third class of British SSNs was the Swiftsure, the first boat joining the fleet in April 1973. These boats are 13ft (4m) shorter than the Valiants with a flat upper deck which gives a completely different appearance from the humped back of the earlier British SSNs. This new shape is evidence of greater internal volume of the pressure hull, giving more equipment space and better living conditions. The fin is

Top: HMS *Swiftsure,* name ship of the third class of SSNs built for the Royal Navy, commissioned on 17 April 1973.

Above: Six Swiftsures were in service by 1981—at an annual running cost (1976 rates) of £3.8 million for each boat.

Left: HMS *Swiftsure* was built by Vickers, Barrow-in-Furness, in 1969-73, at a total cost (1976 rates) of £37.1 million.

lower than on the earlier boats; the diving planes are set very much lower and are not visible when the boat is on the surface. There are five torpedo tubes with twenty reloads. The next type of British SSN is the Trafalgar class, the first of which was launched in 1981. Four are on order, the first of them being the replacement for the Royal Navy's first SSN, HMS *Dreadnought*.

The cost of these SSNs is a good indicator of the problem facing all Western navies. At 1976 prices the building costs of the individual Swiftsures were: *Swiftsure*, £37.1 million; *Superb*, £41.3 million; *Sceptre*, £58.9 million; *Spartan*, £68.9 million. The cost of the fourth of the Trafalgars, including weapons systems and equipment, will be £175 million!

Below: HMS *Superb* (S-109), the third of the Swiftsure class SSNs to be commissioned on 13 November 1976, is seen in the calm waters of the Gareloch, with crewmen lining the casing, as she leaves the Clyde submarine base in March 1978. The 'humped back' of the earlier British SSNs is absent from the Swiftsures, and the diving planes, being set very much lower, are not visible when the boats are surfaced. They have one fewer torpedo tube that the Valiant class that immediately preceded them: each Swiftsure has five 21in (533mm) tubes for the Mark 24 (Modified) Tigerfish, with 20 reloads. Primarily an anti-submarine weapon, but with anti-ship capability, Tigerfish has a range of around 20 miles (32km).

Above: Thirteen feet (4m) shorter than the Valiants, but only about 1ft (0.3m) less in beam, the Swiftsure class hull provides more equipment space and greater habitability.

Below left and right: Swiftsure class SSNs getting under way; note crewmen at work on the flat upper deck.

Far right: The French SSN *Rubis* undergoing sea trials.

Rubis Class (SNA72)

Total built:	One (+three).
Launched:	1979-1984.
Status:	One on trials, remainder building.
Displacement:	2,385 tons (surfaced); 2,670 tons (submerged).
Dimensions:	Length, 236ft 6in (72.1m); beam, 24ft 11 (7.6m); draught, 21ft (6.4m).
Torpedo tubes:	Four 21in (533mm).
Missiles:	Tube-launched SM39.
Propulsion:	Nuclear (48MW).
Shafts:	One.
Speed:	25kt, 46km/hr (submerged).
Complement:	66.

The USA, USSR and UK developed their nuclear-powered submarine fleets first with SSNs and graduated to SSBNs, because missile technology lagged behind that for propulsion systems. France, however, came late to the scene and, under strong pressure from President de Gaulle, the French Navy went straight to SSBNs. Not surprisingly, such a massive programme, which for political reasons had to be entirely French in character, took up all available resources for many years. It was not until the 1974 programme, therefore, that the French Navy was able to turn its attention to SSNs. The first of class, *Rubis* (S-601), was laid down in December 1976 and launched on 7 July 1979. She joins the fleet in 1982, following extensive trials.

The Rubis class (also known as SNA72) are the smallest SSNs in any navy and are based fairly closely on the Agosta class conventional submarines. Such a reduction in size indicates that the French have achieved dramatic developments in nuclear reactor design, compared with the rather large devices in the Le Redoutable class SSBNs.

Armament, sonar and fire control systems are based on those currently in service in the Agosta class and, as with those boats, the torpedo tubes are the internationally standardised 21in (533mm), indicating a final abandonment of the 21.7in (550mm) torpedo. From 1985 onward the Rubis class will be fitted for the SM39, an adaptation of the very successful MM38 Exocet surface-launched anti-ship missile. Like the US Harpoon, SM39 will be tube-launched from the submarine while it is submerged.

Conventional Submarines

During the early 1950s naval pundits were forecasting that the days of the diesel-electric submarine were numbered, and that all future boats, at least in the major navies, would be nuclear-powered. Even some smaller European navies (such as the Royal Netherlands Navy) seriously contemplated nuclear propulsion, while both the US Navy and the Royal Navy committed themselves publicly to all-nuclear submarine fleets. Matters have, however, worked out somewhat differently, and diesel-electric submarines remain in virtually every fleet. Only the US Navy has attained a virtually all-nuclear status, although the French have recently committed themselves to such a goal. The USSR never announced any intentions one way or the other, but it firmly retains several hundred conventional submarines in service and still has conventional production lines. The British, who once wished to go all-nuclear, have 16 conventional boats still in service and recently announced plans to begin construction of a new class (Vickers Type 2400) at a rate of one submarine per year.

The fact is that the modern conventional submarine still has certain advantages to offer, not least of which is economy. The two Los Angeles class SSNs constructed in FY82 will cost $495.8 million each; the British Trafalgar class cost £175 million each at 1981 prices. These are admittedly large and sophisticated deep-ocean boats, but the costs are indicative of the colossal expense involved; only one or two navies can dream of expenditure of that order. A second factor is that SSNs require large crews *(Los Angeles:* 127; *Swiftsure:* 97), whereas the conventional submarine, although admittedly generally smaller, demands far fewer highly-skilled men to operate it (Type 209: 33; Vickers Type 2400: 46).

Nuclear submarines are very powerful and capable of great speeds (over 40 knots in some cases); further, their endurance is only really limited by the stamina of the crew. SSNs cannot, however, avoid making a certain degree of noise which renders them liable to detection, particularly within the confines of the Continental Shelf. Conventional boats are very much quieter when running on their electric motors and are therefore much more suitable for patrol and reconnaissance operations, particularly clandestine missions. (An excellent example of this was afforded by the Soviet Whiskey class submarine which ran aground in Swedish territorial waters in November 1981 while undertaking a surveillance mission outside the Karlskrona Naval Base.) They are, of course, limited by battery life, and when surfacing or 'snorting' to run their diesels are liable to detection. On balance, however, the conventional submarine still has a place in every naval inventory except, apparently, those of the United States of America and France.

Design Innovations

There have been two really important advances in submarine design in the past forty years. The first was the Type XXI, a German design which appeared in 1944. This had a cleaned-up hull in which virtually all of the many projections (guns, bollards, hand-rails, etc) were eliminated, or, in the case of the fin, streamlined. This, coupled with more powerful batteries, led to much greater submerged speeds. This design was the basis of the majority of the early post-war designs in both East and West (eg, Soviet Whiskey and Zulu classes, French Narval class, and the US Guppy conversions).

The next major advance in hull design came with USS *Albacore,* which had a 'tear-drop' shaped hull for even greater hydrodynamic

Above: Of the sixteen conventional submarines now in British service, *Porpoise*, commissioned 17 April 1958, is the veteran.

efficiency, a much finer fin and a single, slow-revving propeller. Control was effected by means of hydrovanes on the fin and a cruciform combination of rudder and hydrovanes at the stern, just in front of the propeller. These measures resulted in a vessel capable of over 30 knots submerged, which effectively outpaced any surface vessel likely to be deployed in an ASW role. As with the Type XXI, the major features of the Albacore design have been copied in virtually every subsequent design.

Conventional submarine development is now at a most interesting stage, with many existing boats in numerous navies becoming due for replacement, notably the ex-US Balao/Tench/Guppy types, the British Porpoise/Oberons and the Soviet Whiskeys and Romeos. There are numerous designs in production (UK: Type 2400; France: Agosta; Italy: Sauro; USSR: Tango; Holland: Walrus; Germany: Type 209, etc) of which the French and German designs have so far proved the most successful in the export market. The British Type 2400 is undoubtedly the most sophisticated of these designs and will probably be the most combat-effective and versatile; unfortunately, it will almost certainly prove far too expensive for most navies. For once the USA finds itself with absolutely nothing that it is able to offer.

Boats in Service

Conventional submarines in service fall into three main categories. The first is the 400-600 ton coastal or shallow-water submarine, which is epitomised by the German Type 205/206 and the Italian Toti

105

classes. These have proved effective little boats, but obviously suffer from limitations in range, torpedo reloads and sensor capacity. The next size is the 900-1,300 ton range, which includes the German Type 209, the Yugoslavian Sava and the Swedish Näcken and Sjöormen classes. These, too, are limited in endurance and carrying capacity and are to be found in the smaller navies with medium-range roles. The majority of current types lie in the 1,600 ton-plus bracket (eg, Japanese Uzushio and Yuushio classes, British Type 2400, Dutch Walrus, Soviet Foxtrot), with the Soviet Tango class of 3,700 tons at the top end of the range.

One of the most significant current developments is the rapid increase in the number of countries capable of manufacturing their own submarines. The traditional manufacturers have been the UK, USSR, USA, France, Germany, Italy, Japan and Sweden; these have now been joined by Argentina, Turkey, Yugoslavia, Denmark, Spain, China and North Korea.

The principal problem still facing the conventional submarine is that of underwater endurance. The streamlined hull and much improved batteries have certainly increased submerged performance, but all must still regularly go to schnorkel depth in order to run their diesels and recharge their batteries. Obviously, this greatly

increases the possibility of detection. The Walter hydrogen-peroxide system had not been perfected by the end of World War II and costly follow-on research programmes in the UK and USSR failed to result in an operational design. It may well be that the concept should now be re-examined in the light of another 30 years' technological progress. Alternatively, the fuel-cell may have reached the stage where its use in submarines is practicable. If the conventional submarine can be freed from regular reliance on approaching the surface—and provided the solution is reasonably cheap—then it should apparently be able to realize its full potential.

Top left: German-built Type 209 (IK62; or Type 1200) diesel-electric boat *Islay* **(S-45), in service with Peruvian Navy.**

Top right: *Nazario Sauro* **was commissioned in 1980, name-boat of a four-strong hunter-killer class for the Italian Navy.**

Bottom left: This Soviet Whiskey patrol submarine was photographed by an RN frigate in the English Channel, 1974.

Bottom right: Converted to Guppy II standard and transferred to Brazil, ex-USS *Grampus* **(SS-523) is seen here in 1972 as** *Rio Grande do Sul.*

Delfinen Class

Total built:	Four.
Launched:	1956-63.
Status:	Four in service.
Displacement:	595 tons (surfaced); 643 tons (submerged).
Dimensions:	Length, 177ft 2in (54m); beam, 15ft 5in (4.7m); draught, 13ft 1in (4m).
Torpedo tubes:	Four 21in (533mm).
Propulsion:	Diesel, two (1,200bhp); electric, two (1,200hp).
Shafts:	Two.
Speed:	16kt, 30km/hr (surfaced); 16kt, 30km/hr (submerged).
Complement:	33.

The Delfinen class submarines were the first to be designed and built in Denmark after World War II. Contemporary with the French Aréthuse class, the Delfinen boats are also similar in operational concept and size. The principal difference is that the Danish boats have twin screws and the French have only one. Significantly, the Danes did not try to design their own replacements for the Delfinens, opting instead to produce their own version of the German Type 205. It is understood that the next boats to be built will be based on the German Type 210: these would replace the Delfinens, which are now more than 20 years old and of limited operational value in the face of the potential enemy.

Above: Delfinen class diesel-electric submarine *Springeren* (S-329), built at the Royal Dockyard, Copenhagen, 1961-63.

Below: *Springeren* under way with crew member on the casing; note that safety lines are rigged along the boat's length.

Narval Class/Aréthuse Class/ Daphné Class

Total built:	Narval: 6; Aréthuse: 3; Daphné: 25.
Launched:	Narval: 1954-58; Aréthuse: 1955-58; Daphné: 1959-67.
Status:	Narval: 6 in service; Aréthuse: 1 in service, 2 in reserve; Daphné: 23 in service.
Displacement:	Narval: 1,635 tons (surfaced.), 1,910 tons (sub); Aréthuse: 543 tons (surfaced), 669 tons (submerged); Daphné: 869 tons (surfaced), 1,043 tons (submerged).
Dimensions:	Narval: length, 254ft 7in (77.6m); beam, 25ft 7in (7.8m); draught, 17ft 8in (5.4m). Aréthuse: length, 162ft 8in (49.6m); beam 19ft (5.8m); draught, 13ft 1in (4m). Daphné: length, 189ft 7in (57.8m); beam, 22ft 4in (6.8m); draught, 15ft 1in (4.6m).

Torpedo tubes:	Narval: six 21.7in (550mm); Aréthuse: four 21.7in (550mm); Daphné: twelve 21.7in (550mm).
Propulsion:	Narval: diesel, three (4,000bhp); electric, two (2,400shp). Aréthuse: diesel, three (1,060bhp); electric, two (1,300shp). Daphné: diesel, three (1,300bhp); electric, two (1,600shp).
Shafts:	Narval: two; Aréthuse: one; Daphné: two.
Speed:	Narval: 15kt, 28km/hr (surfaced), 18kt, 33km/hr (submerged); Aréthuse: 12.5kt, 23km/hr (surfaced), 16kt, 30km/hr (submerged); Daphné: 13.5kt, 25km/hr (surfaced), 16kt, 30km/hr (submerged).
Complement:	Narval: 63; Aréthuse: 40; Daphné: 45.

**Below: This Daphné class submarine is the Spanish Navy's
Delfin (S-61), seen here running trials in 1973. Four
Daphnés were constructed, with French assistance, from
1968 onward by Bazán, Cartagena. The Spanish Daphnés
carry no torpedo reloads but have minelaying capacity.**

Following World War II, the French Navy had some fourteen different types of submarine in service, ranging in size from ocean-going types to midgets. One of these was an ex-German Type XXI (*U-2518*) taken over in 1945 and renamed *Roland Morillot* (S-613). An improved version of this design was produced in France as the Narval class; six were built in the early 1950s and rebuilt in the 1960s, and all are still in service. These boats displace 1,910 tons submerged and are armed with six bow-mounted torpedo tubes. The youngest hull is now some 24 years old, however, and there can only be a few years' service left for this class.

The next class to appear was the Aréthuse, small hunter-killers, of which four were built between 1955 and 1958. They are armed with four bow-mounted torpedo tubes, firing homing torpedoes. Only one remains in service—*Argonaute* (S-636)—and two are in reserve.

Following the success of the Aréthuse class, the French produced a somewhat enlarged version, displacing 1,043 tons submerged, designated the Daphné class. Careful attention was paid to silence of

operation; the exterior shape of the hull was tank-tested in great detail and all mooring equipment is retractable. There are even microphones around the hull which enable those inside to monitor noise-levels and to regulate speed or manoeuvre accordingly.

The Daphné class was an immediate success and eleven entered service with the French Navy between 1964 and 1970. A further ten were sold overseas (South Africa, three; Pakistan, three; Portugal, four) and four were constructed in Spain. In 1968, however, *Minerve* disappeared without trace in the Mediterranean, followed in 1970 by *Eurydice*. These two mysterious losses were nearly followed in 1971 by the *Flore,* when the schnorkel sprang a leak due to a faulty valve; but on this occasion an alert captain took immediate remedial action and managed to save his boat. There have been no further losses, but nor have there been more orders.

Below: *Daphné,* name-boat of a class of 23 patrol submarines (25 built; 2 lost) currently in service with five navies.

Agosta Class

Total built:	Eight (+two).
Launched:	1974-?
Status:	Six in service; four under construction.
Displacement:	1,450 tons (surfaced); 1,725 tons (submerged).
Dimensions:	Length, 221ft 8in (67.6m); beam, 22ft 4in (6.8m); draught, 17ft 8in (5.4m).
Torpedo tubes:	Four 21in (533mm).
Propulsion:	Diesel, two (3,600bhp); electric, one (4,600hp).
Shafts:	One.
Speed:	12kt, 22km/hr (surfaced); 20kt, 37km/hr (submerged).
Complement:	52.

The first of the Agosta class joined the French fleet in 1977 and has since been joined by three more, completing the French Navy's own order for this class. Four Agostas are being built in Spain: two have been completed and the last will be commissioned in 1984. Two of this class have also been built in France for the Pakistan Navy. South Africa also wished to order two Agostas, but this was frustrated by political pressure. Egypt is understood to have made enquiries about purchasing two Agostas, but no order has been announced.

The Agosta class is somewhat larger than the previous Daphné class and is intended for distant water operations. Great attention has been paid to silent operating. Only four torpedo tubes are fitted, but with 20 reloads and special devices for rapid reloading. The torpedo tubes are 21in (533mm) diameter; this is the first time that the French have broken away from their 21.7in (550mm) pattern and is presumably intended to enhance the export prospects of the type. A further unusual feature is the fitting of a small 30hp electric motor for very quiet, low-speed cruising while on patrol.

If the French Navy maintains its announced intention to concentrate on nuclear-powered submarines in future, the Agosta class will be the last of a distinguished line of French conventional boats.

Top: French diesel-electric patrol submarine *Agosta*, name-boat of a class under construction from 1972 onward. The four built for the French Navy are now in service; construction for other navies meanwhile continues.

Above: Note the clean line of *Agosta's* casing; this is one indication of the great design attention—also including internal damping and provision of a supplementary 30hp electric motor—to quietness.

Left: The provision of four 21in (533mm) bow torpedo tubes in the Agosta class—rather than the 21.7in (550mm) pattern previously favoured by French naval designers—may have enhanced export prospects.

Type 205/Improved Type 205/ Type 207

Total built:	Type 205: 12; Improved Type 205: 2; Type 207: 15.
Launched:	Type 205: 1961-68; Improved Type 205: 1968-69; Type 207: 1964-67.
Status:	Type 205: 6 in service; Improved Type 205: 2 in service (Denmark); Type 207: 15 in service (Norway).
Displacement:	Type 205: 419 tons (surfaced), 450 tons (submerged); Improved Type 205: 420 tons (surfaced), 450 tons (submerged); Type 207: 370 tons (surfaced), 435 tons (submerged).
Dimensions:	Type 205: length, 144ft (43.9m); beam 14ft 11in (4.5m); draught, 14ft (4.3m). Improved Type 205: length, 145ft 4in (44.3m); beam, 14ft 11in (4.5m); draught, 12ft 6in (3.8m). Type 207: length, 149ft (45.4m); beam, 15ft 3in (4.6m); draught, 14ft (4.3m).
Torpedo tubes:	Type 205/Improved Type 205/Type 207: eight 21in (533mm).
Propulsion:	Type 205: diesel, two (1,200bhp); electric, one (1,500bhp). Improved Type 205: diesel, two (1,500bhp); electric, one (1,500bhp). Type 207: diesel, two (1,200bhp); electric, one (1,200bhp).
Shafts:	Type 205/Improved Type 205/Type 207: one.
Speed:	Type 205: 10kt, 18.5km/hr (surfaced), 17kt, 31km/hr (submerged); Improved Type 205: 12kt, 22km/hr (surfaced), 17kt, 31km/hr (submerged); Type 207: 10kt, 18.5km/hr (surfaced), 17kt, 31km/hr (submerged).
Complement:	Type 205: 22; Improved Type 205: 22; Type 207: 18.

Germany has had a prominent place in the history of the submarine. She ended World War II with some outstanding designs which, fortunately for the Allies, failed to attain operational status in significant numbers. Following the war there was a total cessation of any submarine activity, but after Germany's admission to NATO in 1954 it was agreed that small coastal boats not exceeding 350 tons displacement would be permitted for use in the Baltic. Design work quickly began on a submarine designated Type 201, but the first boat (*U-1*) was not launched until October 1961.

Meanwhile the Bundesmarine urgently needed to train U-boat crews, but was unable to obtain anything suitable from its NATO allies. It therefore raised three wartime U-boats which had been scuttled in 1945; after reconstruction and refurbishment, these played a valuable

Above right: Type 205 diesel-electric boat *U-12*, launched 1968.

Right: Type 205 boat *U-4*, now no longer in service with the FGN.

role in re-establishing the U-boat arm. The boats concerned were two Type XXIIIs—*Hai* (S-170; ex *U-2365*) and *Hecht* (S-171; ex *U-2367*)—and one Type XXI, *Wilhelm Bauer* (Y-880, ex *U-2540).*

During construction of the Type 201s, the tonnage limit was raised to 450 tons, but in the event these boats, now redesignated Type 205, had a surfaced displacement of 419 tons. These submarines were made of a special non-magnetic steel: there was a major scandal when it transpired that *U-1* and *U-2* were so affected by corrosion that they had to be taken out of service. Two new boats, also designated *U-1* and *U-2*, were built as replacements, but in conventional magnetic steel, and were followed by four more (*U-9* to *U-12*) in a different and more thoroughly tested non-magnetic steel. One boat of this class (*U-3*) was lent to Norway in 1962 and returned in 1964. Only the second *U-1* and *U-2*, together with *U-9* to *U-12*, now remain in service.

Two boats known as the Improved Type 205 were built in Denmark as the Narvhalen class. They have been satisfactory in service, and Denmark is currently planning to build six Type 210s.

The Norwegian Navy expressed an early interest in the Type 205: a construction programme resulted, with the USA paying half the cost. The design selected was the Improved Type 205, but optimised for deep diving. This boat, the Type 207 was made of high-tension steel and has a slightly greater length and diameter than the earlier design. The fin shape is also slightly different. In its main essentials, however, the design is identical with the Type 205; fifteen were built in Germany and all are still in service with the Norwegian Navy.

Type 206/IKL 540

Total built:	Type 206: 18; IKL 540: 3.
Launched:	Type 206: 1971-74; IKL 540: 1975-76.
Status:	Type 206: 18 in service; IKL 540: 3 in service (Israel).
Displacement:	Type 206: 450 tons (surfaced), 498 tons (submerged); IKL 540: 420 tons (surfaced), 600 tons (submerged).
Dimensions:	Type 206: length, 159ft 5in (48.6m); beam, 15ft 1in (4.6m); draught, 14ft 10in (4.5m). IKL 540: length, 146ft 8in (44.7m); beam, 15ft 5in (4.7m); draught, 12ft (3.7m).
Torpedo tubes:	Type 206/IKL 540: eight 21in (533mm).
Propulsion:	Type 206: diesel, two (1,500bhp); electric, one (1,800hp). IKL 540: diesel, two (2,000bhp); electric, one (1,800hp).
Shafts:	Type 206/IKL 540: one.
Speed:	Type 206: 10kt, 18.5km/hr (surfaced), 17kt, 31km/hr (submerged); IKL 540: 11kt, 20km/hr (surfaced), 17kt, 31km/hr (submerged).
Complement:	Type 206: 22; IKL 540: 22.

Following completion of twelve Type 201 and Type 205 boats, design work began on a follow-on class of 450-ton submarines. The main concern was with greater battery power, to meet the demands of ever-increasing numbers of electronic devices without reducing submerged speed or endurance. The opportunity was also taken to update active and passive sonars and fire-control systems. Wire-guided torpedoes were fitted for the first time in a German submarine design.

Above right: *U-13* **(S-192), a Type 206 boat with hull of high-tensile non-magnetic steel.**

Right: Type 206 submerges: periscope, snort induction mast, radar antenna visible.

Below: An unwontedly peaceful setting for two Type 206 patrol boats of the FGN.

Construction of the first boat *(U-13)* began in November 1969; it was launched in September 1971 and the eighteenth and last boat joined the Bundesmarine in March 1974. No further Type 206 boats have been constructed in German yards. Made of special non-magnetic steel, these submarines have served the German Navy well, and so far as is known, have totally avoided the corrosion problems that affected the early Type 205s so badly.

In 1972 a cooperation agreement enabled the British Vickers Shipbuilding Group to construct submarines under licence from Ingenieurkontor Lübeck (IKL), but fitted with British weapons systems. The only known fruit of this agreement was three IKL 540 boats for Israel. Described variously as an adaptation of the Type 206 or as a smaller Type 209, the IKL 540 is optimised for operations in the warmer waters of the eastern Mediterranean. A unique fitting in this type is the fin-mounted SLAM, a quadruple Blowpipe SAM installation, giving the Israeli submarines an anti-aircraft capability. No further orders have been placed with Vickers.

Type 209

Total built:	27 (+13).
Launched:	1970-?
Status:	27 in service; 13 on order.
Displacement:	1,100 tons (surfaced); 1,210 tons (submerged), with minor variations (see text).
Dimensions:	Length, 178ft 5in (54.4m); beam, 20ft 4in (6.2m); draught, 17ft 11in (5.5m), with minor variations (see text).
Torpedo tubes:	Eight 21in (533mm).
Propulsion:	Diesel, four MTU (7,040KW); electric, one Siemens (3,070KW).
Shafts:	One.
Speed:	11kt, 20km/hr (surfaced); 23kt, 43km/hr (submerged).
Complement:	33.

On completion of production of the Types 205 and 207, German yards were faced with a shortage of work, but the raising of the displacement limit to 1,000 tons opened the possibility of a wider export market. This was especially fortunate timing, for many smaller navies were starting to look for a new submarine, conventionally powered and armed,but with up-to-date sensors and electronics, and with minimal demands for highly skilled crews. The Type 209 fitted these requirements almost exactly and some 40 have been ordered.

Greece was the first country to place an order. With the design number IK36, they are known in the Greek Navy as the Glavkos class. The first four were delivered in 1971-72 and a follow-up order for another four was placed in the mid-1970s, with delivery in 1979-80. All eight were built by Howaldtswerke, Kiel.

A new version of the Type 209 then appeared which was 5ft 3in (1.6m) longer. This was ordered by Argentina (two type IK68), Peru (two type IK62 with 35-man crews), Colombia (two type IK78 with 35-man crews) and Turkey (two type IK14 with 33-man crews). An improved version (type IK81), 195ft 2in (59.5m) long and with a large detection dome in the bow, has been ordered by Venezuela (two), Ecuador (two), Turkey (one), Greece (four), Peru (six) and Indonesia (two). Iran also placed an order but this was cancelled after the fall of the Shah. Current unfulfilled orders include another two for Indonesia and two for Venezuela Turkey, having received three from Howaldtswerke, is now producing her own Type 209s; two have been completed and a further seven are planned.

The Type 209 is similar in shape and layout to the Type 205, but has increased dimensions, greater battery capacity and more powerful propulsion. The hull is completely smooth, with retractable hydroplanes mounted low on the bows, cruciform after control surfaces, and a single screw. Careful hull design and powerful motors result in an astonishing underwater 'burst' speed of 23 knots. Designed for patrols lasting up to 50 days, these boats are armed with eight 21in (533mm) torpedo tubes and have a full array of sensors. They must rate as one of the most successful of contemporary submarine designs: Ingenieurkontor Lübeck have obviously assessed potential customers' requirements with a remarkable degree of accuracy.

Below left: A Type 209 built for export by Howaldtswerke, Kiel, flies the German Federal Republic flag while on trial.

Below centre: Type 209 at extreme trim during sea training (upper) and seen bow on while under way on surface (lower).

Below right: Type 209 under construction, displaying its single screw and cruciform after control surfaces.

Enrico Toti Class

Total built:	Four.
Launched:	1967-68.
Status:	Four in service.
Displacement:	524 tons (surfaced); 582 tons (submerged).
Dimensions:	Length, 151ft 6in (46.2m); beam, 15ft 5in (4.7m); draught, 13ft 1in (4m).
Torpedo tubes:	Four 21in (533mm).
Propulsion:	Diesel, two (2,200bhp); electric, one (2,200bhp).
Shafts:	One.
Speed:	14kt, 26km/hr (surfaced); 15kt, 28km/hr (submerged).
Complement:	26.

The Italian Navy's first post-war submarines were the four boats of the Enrico Toti class. Italy's post-war force began with three wartime submarines (two Flutto and one Acciaio class), followed by five modernized Gato and Balao class boats acquired from the USA. Although sound designs, especially after modernization, these ex-US boats are somewhat large for Mediterranean operations.

The operational requirement for the Totis changed several times, and the design was recast accordingly before being finalised as a coastal hunter/killer. Since the Totis are intended for the shallow and confined waters of the central Mediterranean and the Adriatic, their restricted surface range is no handicap and size has been kept to a minimum. They are small and highly manoeuvrable, with a 'teardrop' hull and a single screw. They have diesel-electric drive and diving depth is 600ft (180m). The active sonar is in a prominent dome on the bow, while the passive sonar is contained in the stern. The four torpedo tubes are also mounted in the bow. The Enrico Toti class makes an interesting comparison with the German Types 205 and 206: it is noteworthy that the Italian design never won any export orders.

Below centre: Small and manoeuvrable, the Totis are well suited to operations in the Mediterranean and Adriatic.

Below: The prominent dome on the bow of the _Enrico Toti,_ name-boat of a hunter-killer class, houses the active sonar.

Nazario Sauro Class

Total built:	Four.
Launched:	1976-82.
Status:	Four in service.
Displacement:	1,456 tons (surfaced); 1,631 tons (submerged).
Dimensions:	Length, 210ft (64m); beam, 22ft 6in (6.8m); draught, 18ft 10in (5.7m).
Torpedo tubes:	Six 21in (533mm).
Propulsion:	Diesel, three (3,210bhp); electric, one (3,650hp).
Shafts:	One.
Speed:	11kt, 20km/hr (surfaced); 20kt, 37km/hr (submerged).
Complement:	45.

The Nazario Sauro class of four submarines is built by the Monfalcone yard of Italcantieri, the only Italian producer of submarines. The Sauros are the largest submarines produced in Italy since World War II, but, even so, at 1,631 tons submerged they are somewhat smaller than the ex-US boats they are replacing. The hull is an Albacore-type tear-drop shape with cruciform after control surfaces and a very large, slow-turning seven-bladed screw. The forward control surfaces are mounted, American fashion, on the fin.

The Sauro class have six bow-mounted torpedo tubes with six reloads: a total of only 12 torpedoes seems a little inadequate for such a large boat designed for 45-day patrols. The French Agosta class, for example, with a similar size and displacement, carries 16 reloads for its four tubes, a total of 20 torpedoes.

Many navies are looking for replacements for their conventional submarines in the 1,000 to 2,000 ton displacement bracket, but whereas orders have been placed for the German Type 209, the French Agosta and the Dutch Zwaardvis designs, none has yet been placed for the Sauro. Most noteworthy is the fact that when Greece and Turkey were looking for submarines to use in the Mediterranean they selected the Type 209 in preference to the Sauro, although the latter had presumably been optimised for Mediterranean conditions.

Below right: Stern view of *Nazario Sauro* before launching shows seven-bladed screw and cruciform after control surfaces.

Ooshio Class/Uzushio Class/ Yuushio Class

Total built:	Ooshio: 5; Uzushio: 7; Yuushio: 2 (+3).
Launched:	Ooshio: 1963-67: Uzushio: 1970-77; Yuushio: 1979-83.
Status:	Ooshio: 5 in service: Uzushio: 7 in service; Yuushio: 2 in service, 3 on order.
Displacement:	Ooshio: 1,650 tons (surfaced); Uzushio: 1,850 tons (surfaced); Yuushio: 2,200 tons (surfaced).
Dimensions:	Ooshio: length, 288ft 8in (88m); beam, 26ft 11in (8.2m); draught, 16ft 2in (4.9m). Uzushio: length, 236ft 2in (72m); beam, 29ft 6in (9m); draught, 24ft 7in (7.5m). Yuushio: length, 249ft 4in (76m); beam, 32ft 6in (9.9m); draught, 24ft 7in (7.5m).
Torpedo tubes:	Ooshio: six 21in (533mm) bow, two 12.7in (322mm) stern; Uzushio/Yuushio: six 21in (533mm) amidships.
Propulsion:	Ooshio: diesel, two (2,900bhp); electric, two (6,300hp). Uzushio: diesel, two (3,400bhp); electric, one (7,200hp). Yuushio: diesel, two (4,200bhp); electric, one (7,200hp).
Shafts:	Ooshio: two; Uzushio/Yuushio: one.
Speed:	Ooshio: 14kt, 26km/hr (surfaced), 18kt, 33km/hr (submerged); Uzushio/Yuushio: 12kt, 22km/hr (surfaced), 20kt, 37km/hr (submerged).
Complement:	Ooshio: 80; Uzushio: 80; Yuushio: 75.

Having begun its post-war reconstruction with ex-US submarines, the Japanese Maritime Self-Defense Force (JMSDF) produced its first indigenous design, the Oyashio class, in 1959. The design was refined and improved, leading to the four-boat Hayashio class launched in 1961-62. All these boats have now been stricken, but the culmination of this line of development—the Ooshio class—is still in service. This is a neat and workmanlike design, with the now somewhat unusual feature of twin 12.7in (322mm) stern torpedo tubes.

The next class, Uzushio, was based on the US Navy's Barbel design, with an Albacore-type 'tear-drop' hull for faster and quieter underwater performance. The hull was built of very high quality steel to permit a diving depth of up to 650ft (198m).

The latest Japanese submarines are those of the Yuushio class, which is basically an all-round improvement on the Uzushio class, capable of slightly higher speeds. Both the Uzushio and Yuushio class submarines have their torpedo tubes mounted amidships, a feature they share with the US Navy's SSNs. This frees the entire bow area for a large sonar array. The tubes are canted outwards at an angle of 10°.

The Uzushio class have pressure hulls of NS-63 high-tensile steel, which permits a maximum diving depth of 1,970ft (600m). The Yuushios' hulls are of even more modern steel (NS-90), giving a claimed diving depth of 3,280ft (1,000m). The first two Yuushios will be retro-fitted to take Sub-Harpoon missiles; the remaining boats of the class will be fitted for the missiles prior to delivery. These Japanese submarines are very advanced, as one would expect from such a technologically capable nation, and would seem to be equivalent to SSNs in most features—except the crucial one of underwater endurance. This may drive the JMSDF towards seeking a solution to the problem of freeing the diesel-electric submarine from the necessity to come up to 'breathe' at regular intervals.

Below: The sleek lines of the Albacore-derived 'tear-drop' hull of the Uzushio class are well displayed in this photograph of the submarine *Isoshio* running trials in 1972.

Dolfijn Class

Total built:	Four.
Launched:	1959-65.
Status:	Four in service.
Displacement:	1,494 tons (surfaced); 1,826 tons (submerged).
Dimensions:	Length, 260ft 11in (79.5m); beam, 25ft 10in (7.8m); draught, 16ft 5in (5m).
Torpedo tubes:	Eight 21in (533mm) (four bow, four stern).
Propulsion:	Diesel, two (3,100bhp); electric, two (4,200hp).
Shafts:	One.
Speed:	14.5kt, 27km/hr (surfaced); 17kt, 31.5km/hr (submerged).
Complement:	67.

The Dutch have a well-deserved reputation for innovative submarine design. It was, for example, a Dutch naval officer who invented the schnorkel tube, as a means of ventilating a submerged submarine in the East Indies, in the mid-1930s. When, therefore, they decided to build their first class of post-war boats, it is not surprising that they once again came up with an unusual, indeed unique, concept.

A new class of four boats was authorized in 1949, but the first pair *(Dolfijn* and *Tonijn)* were delayed pending a decision on whether they should be nuclear-powered. Finally, following the realization that this would be prohibitively expensive, the last two boats were laid down in

1962 and completed in 1965-66. Naturally this second pair incorporated improvements, and they were, for some time, considered to be a separate class. Since then, however, various refits have led to all four boats being virtually identical.

The outstanding feature of the Dolfijn boats is that instead of having the usual single pressure hull of a normal submarine, they have three separate though interconnected pressure hulls in a 'treble-bubble' arrangement. The uppermost (and largest) contains the crew and most of the equipment, while below it and alongside each other are two smaller hulls, each containing machinery and stores. The advantage of this odd layout is that it gives increased strength and compactness, although this tends to be offset by the very cramped conditions in the two lower hulls, which make machinery maintenance and repair very difficult. This, combined with the increased complexity and greater manufacturing costs, appears to have deterred the Dutch from further development of this interesting idea: their latest submarines have reverted to the conventional single pressure hull. The triple hull arrangement, however, has allowed a diving depth of 980ft (300m); its streamlining gives an excellent submerged performance, and the Dolfijns are very quiet boats.

The two oldest submarines in this class—*Dolfijn* and *Zeehond*—will be paid off when the two Walrus class join the fleet in 1983-84.

Below: Dolfijn class (originally Potvis class) diesel-electric submarine *Potvis* of the Royal Netherlands Navy. These boats are notable for their 'treble-bubble' pressure hulls.

Zwaardvis Class/Walrus Class

Total built:	Zwaardvis: 2; Walrus: (2).
Launched:	Zwaardvis: 1970-71; Walrus: 1982-83.
Status:	Zwaardvis: 2 in service; Walrus: building.
Displacement:	Zwaardvis/Walrus: 2,350 tons (surfaced), 2,640 tons (submerged).
Dimensions:	Zwaardvis: length, 217ft 2in (66.2m); beam, 33ft 10in (10.3m); draught, 23ft 4in (7.1m). Walrus: length, 220ft (67m); beam, 27ft 7in (8.4m); draught, 23ft (7m).
Torpedo tubes:	Zwaardvis/Walrus: six 21in (533mm).
Propulsion:	Zwaardvis: diesel, three (5,200bhp); electric, one. Walrus: diesel, three; electric, one.
Shafts:	Zwaardvis/Walrus: one.
Speed:	Zwaardvis: 13kt, 24km/hr (surfaced); 20kt, 37km/hr (submerged).
Complement:	Zwaardvis: 65; Walrus: 49.

The two boats of the Zwaardvis class are among the largest conventional submarines currently in service: only the US Navy's Barbel class and the Soviet Tangos have comparable displacement. The design

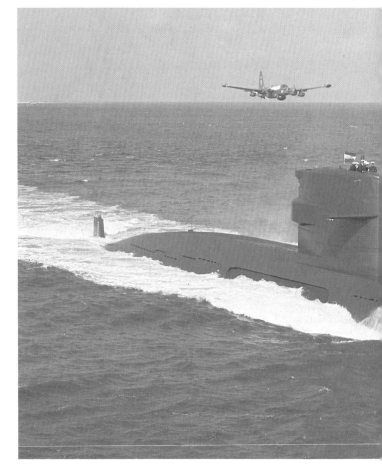

of the Zwaardvis is, in fact, based upon that of the Barbel, with a similar 'Albacore' hull. This type of hull has considerable internal depth, making it possible to have two decks; this gives a generally roomy interior and greatly improves living conditions.

The Zwaardvis boats are obviously capable of protracted operations in the Atlantic, where they would probably operate as part of the task groups which the Royal Netherlands Navy has undertaken to provide as part of its NATO commitment. Three diesel-generators power the propulsion motor for surface running and two groups of batteries provide underwater power. A single five-bladed propeller is mounted abaft the cruciform control surfaces, and a 'burst' speed well in excess of 20 knots is probable.

The Zwaardvis class will be supplemented in the mid-1980s by two improved submarines designated the Walrus class. The dimensions and silhouettes are virtually identical with the Zwaardvis class, but use of the new French 'Marel' high tension steel will increase diving depth by at least 50 per cent. Updated and automated electronics will enable the crew to be reduced from 65 to 49. The two boats so far ordered will replace the *Dolfijn* and *Zeehond* of the Potvis class; two more are planned to replace *Potvis* and *Tonijn* in the late 1980s.

Below: SP-2H Neptune aircraft of the Royal Netherlands Navy comes in low over the large diesel-electric boat *Zwaardvis*.

Sjöormen Class/Näcken Class

Total built:	Sjöormen: 5; Näcken: 3 (+2?).
Launched:	Sjöormen: 1967-68; Näcken: 1978 onward.
Status:	Sjöormen: 5 in service; Näcken: 3 in service.
Displacement:	Sjöormen: 1,125 tons (surfaced), 1,400 tons (submerged); Näcken: 980 tons (surfaced), 1,125 tons (submerged).
Dimensions:	Sjöormen: length, 167ft 4in (51m); beam, 20ft (6.1m); draught, 16ft 8in (5.1m). Näcken: length, 135ft (41.1m); beam, 20ft (6.1m); draught, 13ft 5in (4.1m).
Torpedo tubes:	Sjöormen: four 21in (533mm); Näcken: six 21in (533mm).
Propulsion:	Sjöormen: diesel, two (2,200bhp); electric, one. Näcken: diesel, two (2,300bhp); electric, one.
Shafts:	Sjöormen/Näcken: one.
Speed:	Sjöormen: 15kt, 28km/hr (surfaced), 20kt, 37km/hr (submerged); Näcken: 20kt, 37km/hr (surfaced), 20kt, 37km/hr (submerged).
Complement:	Sjöormen: 23; Näcken: 19.

The five submarines of the Sjöormen class joined the Swedish fleet between 1967 and 1969. The design was based, like so many others, on the revolutionary Albacore hull, as were the indexed cruciform after control surfaces. The large fin towers over the bow; the forward control surfaces are mounted on the fin, rather than in the bows, as is the American practice.

Endurance is estimated to be some three weeks and it is assumed that the class is intended primarily for operations in the Baltic. Normal crew is 23, although operations are possible with only 18. This contrasts dramatically with the 44 required to man the boats of the earlier Draken class.

The Sjöormen class was followed in the late 1970s by the Näcken class. These new boats are capable of operating at depths of up to 984ft (300m) and may be intended to operate ouside the Baltic in the trenches of the Skagerrak. Based on the Sjöormen, the Näcken is a little smaller; very great attention has been paid to quietness and to effective control at slow speeds. Although the third boat of the Näcken class was commissioned in 1979, it is possible that two more may be built before the first of the new A17 type is laid down. Little is known of the A17, except that it is being designed by Kockums of Malmö.

Below: Näcken class diesel-electric boat *Najad* runs trials off Malmö. Like the earlier Sjöormen class—and many other worldwide—the Näcken design is based on the revolutionary Albacore.

Above: *Sjöormen,* name-boat of a class of five currently in service, can be operated by as few as eighteen crewmen.

Below: The Draken class boat *Vargen* entered service in 1961, and, like her five sisters, is now of limited operational value.

Draken Class

Total built:	Six.
Launched:	1960-61.
Status:	Six in service.
Displacement:	835 tons (surfaced); 1,110 tons (submerged).
Dimensions:	Length, 226ft 5in (69m); beam, 16ft 8in (5.1m); draught, 16ft 5in (5m).
Torpedo tubes:	Four 21in (533mm) (bow).
Propulsion:	Diesel, two (1,660hp); electric, one.
Shafts:	One.
Speed:	17kt, 31.5km/hr (surfaced); 20kt, 37km/hr (submerged).
Complement:	44.

Sweden's first post-war submarine design was the Hajen class, which was based very closely on the German Type XXI, although there were a surprising number of protuberances on the upper deck. The six boats of the Hajen class were launched between 1956 and 1960 and have now been scrapped, but they were followed by a derivative known variously as the Hajen class Type B or as the Draken class.

The Draken class has a large single propeller (as opposed to the Hajen's two), cruciform control surfaces and an 11ft (3.35m) increase in length. They are now rather elderly and of limited operational value; they will presumably be replaced by either A14 Näckens or the projected A17 boats in the near future.

Foxtrot Class

Total built:	62+.
Launched:	1958 onward.
Status:	60 in service with USSR; at least 13 exported.
Displacement:	1,950 tons (surfaced); 2,500 tons (submerged).
Dimensions:	Length, 300ft 1in (91.5m); beam, 26ft 2in (8m); draught, 20ft (6.1m).
Torpedo tubes:	Six 21in (533mm) (bow); four 16in (406mm) (stern).
Propulsion:	Diesel, three (6,000bhp); electric, three (6,000hp).
Shafts:	Three.
Speed:	18kt, 33km/hr (surfaced); 16kt, 30km/hr (submerged).
Complement:	75.

These patrol submarines, with conventional diesel-electric propulsion and torpedo armament, have been built in greater numbers than any other single class of submarine since the Soviet Whiskeys. The first Foxtrots appeared around 1958 and remained in production at the rate of about seven per year, from the well-established yards at Sudomekh and Leningrad, until some 62 had been delivered. A slightly larger follow-on to the Zulu class, they are fitted with similar propulsion to the Golf class. It is suggested they were built in three sub-classes, differing in propulsion fits.

By all accounts the Foxtrots have been extremely successful, and they have been encountered frequently by Western aircraft and ships all over the world. Since 1968 many units of this class have been sold or given to other countries, and production for export continues.

Left: Cold work in the Atlantic! Secured by a safety line to the fin of a Foxtrot class patrol submarine, a Soviet Navy diver prepares to go overside to retrieve a sonobuoy dropped by a NATO aircraft. The sixty active boats of the Foxtrot class are frequently encountered worldwide.

Above: The bow sonars (Hercules and Feniks are carried) are particularly clearly seen in this photograph of a Foxtrot boat. The class first went into production in 1958 and is still built for export: Foxtrot boats serve with the navies of Cuba, India and Libya.

Top: Apparently somewhat the worse for wear, a Foxtrot class patrol submarine passes a Soviet guided-missile destroyer of the Kashin class.

Centre: This Foxtrot submarine was spotted by a US Navy aircraft while under way off the coast of Spain, May 1972.

Romeo Class

Total built:	93+
Launched:	1958-61.
Status:	12 in service.
Displacement:	1,400 tons (surfaced); 1,800 tons (submerged).
Dimensions:	Length, 251ft 11in (76.8m); beam, 23ft 11in (7.3m); draught, 18ft (5.5m).
Torpedo tubes:	Eight 21in (533m) (6 bow, 2 stern).
Propulsion:	Diesel, two (4,000bhp); electric, two (4,000hp).
Shafts:	Two.
Speed:	17kt, 31.5km/hr (surfaced); 14kt, 26km/hr (submerged).
Complement:	54.

These patrol submarines were a direct development of the mass-produced Whiskey class; more than 20 were built in Soviet yards in the early 1960s, and production continues in China and North Korea.

The Romeos have hulls which are slightly longer than the Whiskey class, with fractionally greater beam. They have improved electric propulsion, new fins, and—most important of all—a much later and more comprehensive suite of sonar sensor and electronic equipment. They are medium-range vessels and tend to stay relatively close to Soviet shores.

China continues to build Romeo class submarines at a rate of nine per year and has some 68 in service. Seven Romeos were transferred by China to North Korea in the early 1970s, and the latter country has since produced a further five of its own, with production continuing at a slow rate.

Repeated reports refer also to another type of Chinese submarine designated the 'Ming' class. All data so far published are very similar to those given for the Romeo class: it could well be that these 'Ming' boats are simply a Chinese development of the original Soviet design.

Above: Romeo class patrol submarine surfaced in Atlantic.

Bottom left: Romeo class; medium-range diesel-electric boat.

Bottom right: Twelve of the 20-plus Soviet-built Romeos are in service; China has some 68 serving and more building.

Romeo class SS.

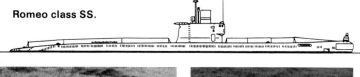

Tango Class

Total built:	15+.
Launched:	1972 onward.
Status:	15+ in service.
Displacement:	3,000 tons (surfaced); 3,700 tons (submerged).
Dimensions:	Length, 301ft 10in (92m); beam, 29ft 6in (9m); draught, 23ft (7m).
Torpedo tubes:	Eight 21in (533mm).
Propulsion:	Diesel, three (6,000shp); electric, three (6,000shp).
Shafts:	Three.
Speed:	20kt, 37km/hr (surfaced); 16kt, 30km/hr (submerged).
Complement:	62.

The Tango class was first seen by Western observers at the Sebastopol Naval Review in July 1973, and production has since continued at a rate of about 2 to 3 boats a year. This class is of advanced design and it is of interest that the USSR does not seem particularly keen to export it, despite the considerable market for a conventionally-powered submarine of this size and capability. It is clearly regarded as complementary to the nuclear SSNs, and could well be intended for use in the extensive shallow waters around the Soviet Union. The continued production of this class makes it clear that the USSR does not intend to follow the USA's example in aiming for an all nuclear-powered submarine fleet.

The hull has very smooth lines, but one noteworthy feature is that forward of the fin there is a marked rise of some 3ft (0.91m). This will undoubtedly improve sea-keeping when on the surface, but also suggests a requirement for extra volume in the forward end of the boat, possibly for some new and advanced weapon system such as SS-N-15. The smooth lines of these submarines suggest a small and compact design, but this is deceptive: they are, in fact, the largest conventional submarines currently in production.

Top: Tango class diesel-electric patrol submarine; possibly intended mainly for shallow-water operations around the USSR.

Above: Seen here dressed overall with the crew lined up on the casing in dress whites, the Tango class was first seen by the West at the Sebastopol Naval Review in July 1973.

Left: The rise of the hull forward of the fin suggests that the Tango may be able to accommodate the SS-N-15 ASW.

Tango class SS.

Whiskey Class

Total built:	Approximately 260.
Launched:	1951-64.
Status:	Approximately 50 in service; 100 in reserve.
Displacement:	1,080 tons (surfaced); 1,350 tons (submerged).
Dimensions:	Length, 249ft 4in (76m); beam, 21ft 4in (6.5m); draught, 16ft 1in (4.9m).
Torpedo tubes:	Four 21in (533mm) (bow); two 16in (406mm) (stern).
Propulsion:	Diesel, two (4,000bhp); electric, two (2,700hp).
Shafts:	Two.
Speed:	18kt, 33km/hr (surfaced); 14kt, 26km/hr (submerged).
Complement:	54.

For one week in November 1981 a Whiskey class submarine attained an unenviable degree of international notoriety after it ran aground while carrying out a clandestine reconnaissance of Sweden's Karlskrona Naval Base. The incident not only illustrated the daring of the Soviets in carrying out such a blatant breach of Sweden's neutrality, but also showed the continuing value of small conventional submarines for such purposes.

The Whiskey class was one of three types based on the German Type XXI designed in the early 1950s. The Zulus were the large, long-range boats; the Quebecs, the small coastal type; and in between came the Whiskeys. The Whiskeys were formidable submarines in their day and the large numbers in which they were built gave a

Above: Whiskey class diesel-electric patrol submarines like that seen here are being phased out of Soviet service. Of some 260 built, about 50 remain operational, with some 100 in reserve.

Below left: Surfaced Whiskey under way. Many of these boats have been transferred to Warsaw Pact and other friendly navies.

Below: Search radar on fin of Whiskey Canvas-Bag conversion.

considerable impetus to the development of a new generation of Western anti-submarine escorts, weapons and techniques. By today's standards, the Whiskeys are noisy and relatively easy to detect; thus, they are being gradually phased out of Soviet service, some 50 remaining operational with about 100 in reserve.

Six known variants of the basic design were produced, most differentiated mainly by the presence or absence of a gun. All those still in Soviet service are the Whiskey V version, to which the data given above apply. The Whiskey Twin Cylinder and the more efficient Whiskey Long-Bin conversions were the first Soviet cruise-missile submarines. The Whiskey Canvas-Bag type is a radar-picket version; only one or two were produced and they are thought to be still in service, although their current operational role is not known.

Many Whiskey class submarines have been exported. Those known still to be in service are: Albania: three; Bulgaria: two; Cuba: one; Egypt: six; Indonesia: two; North Korea: four; Poland: four. Separate production has been undertaken in the People's Republic of China, where 21 are in service.

One of the more surprising revelations in the 'Karlskrona incident', referred to above, was that the Swedish authorities detected nuclear radiation from the bow area of the stranded submarine. This suggests that, old as it is, the Whiskey class is being kept up-to-date with modern weaponry, in this case probably a conventional 21in (533mm) torpedo with a nuclear warhead. The other factor in this discovery is that if the radiation is so easily detected outside the boat, there must be a considerable hazard for the unfortunate crew inside!

Above: This close amidships view of a Whiskey Canvas-Bag radar-picket submarine, obtained by a US Navy aircraft in 1970, clearly shows the large Boat-Sail air search radar aerial that gained these conversions their Western designation. Very few underwent the conversion: one or two are believed to be still in service in an undefined role.

Left: Whiskey on the rocks; Swedish patrol boats alongside the Soviet submarine stranded during a clandestine reconnaissance of Karlskrona Naval Base, November 1981. Detection of nuclear radiation from the bow suggested that the Whiskeys, old as they are, have up-to-date weaponry: in this case, probably a conventional 21in (533mm) torpedo with a nuclear warhead.

Whiskey Canvas-Bag and variant.

Zulu IV Class

Total built:	28.
Launched:	1951-55.
Status:	Twelve in service; seven in reserve.
Displacement:	1,950 tons (surfaced); 2,300 tons (submerged).
Dimensions:	Length, 295ft 2in (90m); beam, 24ft 4in (7.4m); draught, 20ft (6.1m).
Torpedo tubes:	Ten 21in (533mm) (six bow, four stern).
Propulsion:	Diesel, three (10,000shp); electric, three (4,050hp).
Shafts:	Three.
Speed:	18kt, 33km/hr (surfaced); 16kt, 30km/hr (submerged).
Complement:	75.

The Zulu class boats were built as long-range versions of the Whiskey class, and like them were based fairly closely on the German Type XXI. The Zulus have a larger hull than the Whiskeys, with three rather than two shafts and four more torpedo tubes. An improved version, the Foxtrot class, was built between 1958 and 1975, with a longer hull and generally improved performance and capabilities.

Five variants of the basic Zulu design have been identified, four of which differ only in minor details. The Zulu V boats, however, were fitted with a greatly enlarged fin containing two vertical launching tubes outside the pressure hull for SS-N-4 (Sark) SLBMs. These surface-launched missiles had a nuclear warhead, but a range of only 350 miles (563km) made them very susceptible to countermeasures. The Zulu Vs became operational in 1958 and were the USSR's first ballistic missile submarines. All five have long since reverted to other roles: two are patrol submarines and the other three are used as research vessels.

No Zulu class boats have been exported. Twelve remain in Soviet service, with seven in reserve, but it is presumed that all will be stricken in the near future.

Top: Partly-submerged Zulu class patrol submarine, seen in
July 1962. Only 12 of the 28 Zulus built are now in service.

Above: The enlarged fin of a Zulu V conversion, clearly
showing the launching tubes for SS-N-4 (Sark) SLBMs.

Left: Zulu class submarine on patrol, 1979. The Zulu I,
II, III and IV types differ only in minor details.

Zulu III class SS.

Porpoise Class/Oberon Class

Total built:	Porpoise: 8; Oberon: 13.
Launched:	Porpoise: 1956-59; Oberon: 1959-62.
Status:	Porpoise: 3 in service; Oberon: 27 in service.
Displacement:	2,030 tons (surfaced); 2,410 tons (submerged).
Dimensions:	Length, 295ft 2in (90m); beam, 26ft 6in (8.1m); draught, 18ft (5.5m).
Torpedo tubes:	Eight 21in (533m) (6 bow, 2 stern).
Propulsion:	Diesel, two (3,680bhp); electric, two (6,000hp).
Shafts:	Two.
Speed:	12kt, 22km/hr (surfaced); 17kt, 31.5km/hr (submerged).
Complement:	Porpoise: 71; Oberon: 69.

After World War II the Royal Navy ran trials with a number of ex-German submarines, including HMS *Meteorite* (ex *U-1407),* a Walter Type XVIIB, powered by a hydrogen-peroxide fuelled turbine. This was followed by two British-designed and built hydrogen-peroxide fuelled boats, HMS *Explorer* (S-30) and *Excalibur* (S-40) which ran trials between 1956 and 1965 when, to the profound relief of those involved, the project was shelved.

The first British post-war operational boats were the Porpoise class, which combined the best features of conventional British and German wartime designs. They have a semi-streamlined hull and are extremely quiet, with an excellent range and habitability and a deep designed diving depth. Some of the class were discarded before the planned date to permit more men and money to be allocated to the nuclear submarine programme.

The Oberons are virtually a repeat of the Porpoises, but with improved equipment and a glass-fibre superstructure fore and aft of the fin in all except *Orpheus,* which uses light aluminium alloy. A number of these excellent boats have been supplied to other navies: Australia: six; Brazil: three; Canada: three; Chile: two. Thirteen still serve with the Royal Navy, where their replacement is becoming rather critical.

Above: Crewmen at controls of *Porpoise*, name-boat of an eight-strong class dating from the 1950s; three are still in service.

Below: HMS *Otter* (S-15) of the Oberon class; virtually identical with the Porpoises but with improved equipment.

Top: Both Porpoise (seen here) and Oberon class boats mount eight 21in (533mm) torpedo tubes: six bow, two stern. Stern tubes are designed to launch short anti-submarine torpedoes.

Above: A lieutenant at the periscope aboard *Porpoise.* These boats have a designed diving depth of *c*900ft (275m).

Right: Manufacturer's impression of the Vickers Type 2400 diesel-electric boat, on which it is planned the Royal Navy's new conventional patrol submarine will be very closely based.

Vickers Type 2400

Total built:	None.
Launched:	—
Status:	Unspecified number on order for the Royal Navy.
Displacement:	2,125 tons (surfaced); 2,362 tons (submerged).
Dimensions:	Length, 230ft 6in (70.25m); beam, 24ft 11in (7.6m); draught, 24ft 7in (7.5m).
Torpedo tubes:	Six 21in (533mm).
Propulsion:	Diesel, two; electric, one.
Shafts:	One.
Speed:	12kt, 22km/hr (surfaced); 20+kt, 37km/hr (submerged).
Complement:	46.

It is now some 20 years since the final submarine of the Oberon class entered service with the Royal Navy, and it had been intended that that class should be the last of the conventional boats. There is no doubt that the nuclear-powered submarine has many advantages, but the Royal Navy has now accepted that there is still an operational need for the conventional type as well. There is thus an urgent need to replace the Porpoise and Oberon boats: their hulls are all more than 20 years old and the design itself is based on the technology of the early 1950s.

The new Royal Navy conventional patrol submarine will be based very closely upon the Vickers Type 2400, so called because its submerged displacement is 2400 tonnes (2,362 tons). This type will be built at a rate of about one per year and will be a very welcome addition to the fleet. A unit cost of £50 million has been quoted, but it seems likely to be very much more than this.

The Type 2400 will have a tear-drop type hull with cruciform after hydroplanes and retractable forward hydroplanes mounted low on the bow. Many special features have been incorporated into the design to minimise radiated noise and thus achieve a marked reduction in the noise signature. A major factor is the maximum use of manpower-saving devices, reducing the crew to 46 compared to 69 in the Oberons. A diesel-electric propulsion system is fitted, comprising a single fixed-pitch propeller on a shaft directly driven by a twin-armature electric motor. On the surface and when 'snorting', two four-stroke high-speed diesels are used, each driving a 1.25MW AC generator.

The most modern sensors will be fitted, and there will be six torpedo tubes in the bow. These will fire normal torpedoes or Harpoon missiles, or can be used to lay submarine mines.

There is doubtless a large overseas market for this type and size of patrol submarine with countries who wish to replace their Oberons, Guppies and Balaos. For the Type 2400 to obtain a share of this market, the price will have to be right—and this will only be achieved if the degree of sophistication is kept to a reasonable level.

Balao Class/
Guppy Conversions

Total built:	Balao: 119. Guppy 1A: 10; Guppy II: 15; Guppy IIA: 16; Guppy III: 9.
Launched/ converted:	Balao: 1943-48: Guppy IA: 1951; Guppy II: 1948-50; Guppy IIA: 1952-54; Guppy III: 1960-62.
Status:	Balao: 3 active; Guppy IA: 4 active; Guppy II: 7 active; Guppy IIA: 11 active; Guppy III: 6 active.
Displacement:	Balao: 1,450 tons (surfaced); 2,400 tons (submerged). Guppy IA: 1,870 tons (surfaced); 2,440 tons (submerged). Guppy II: 1,870 tons (surfaced); 2,420 tons (submerged). Guppy IIA: 1,840 tons (surfaced); 2,445 tons (submerged). Guppy III: 1,975 tons (surfaced); 2,540 tons (submerged).
Dimensions:	Balao: length, 312ft (95.1m); beam, 27ft 2in (8.3m); draught, 17ft 2in (5.25m). Guppy IA: length, 308ft (93.9m); beam, 27ft (8.2m); draught, 17ft (5.2m). Guppy II: length, 307ft 6in (93.7m); beam, 27ft 2in (8.3m); draught, 18ft (5.5m). Guppy IIA: length, 306ft (93.3m); beam, 27ft (8.2m); draught, 17ft (5.2m). Guppy III: length, 326ft 6in (99.5m); beam, 27ft (8.2m); draught, 17ft (5.2m).
Torpedo tubes:	Balao/Guppy IA/Guppy II/Guppy IIA/Guppy III: ten 21in (533mm); six bow, four stern.
Propulsion:	Balao: diesel, four (6,400shp); electric, two (5,400shp). Guppy IA/II/IIA: diesel, three (4,800shp); electric, two (5,400shp). Guppy III: diesel, four (6,400shp); electric, two (5,400shp).
Shafts:	Balao/Guppy IA/Guppy II/Guppy IIA/Guppy III:two.
Speed:	Balao: 20kt, 37km/hr (surfaced); 10kt, 18.5km/hr (submerged). Guppy IA/Guppy II/Guppy IIA: 18kt, 33km/hr (surfaced); 15kt, 28km/hr (submerged). Guppy III: 20kt, 37km/hr (surfaced); 15kt, 28km/hr (submerged).
Complement:	Balao: 85; Guppy IA: 84; Guppy II: 82; Guppy IIA: 84; Guppy III: 86.

Of the many hundred fleet submarines of World War II, none now remains in service with the US Navy, but some 29 are still active with other navies. In the years 1943-48, 119 Balao class fleet submarines were built, of which only three now remain in service—one with Chile, one with Spain, one with Turkey—all scheduled for replacement in the next few years. These three boats have obviously had some modification since the end of the war, but nothing so drastic as that of the Guppy programme.

Above: Seen here in 1957, the Balao class fleet submarine USS *Menhaden* was converted to Guppy IIA standard in 1952-54.

Following detailed examination of the German Type XXI, the US Navy decided to initiate a rebuilding programme to bring at least part of its large number of fleet submarines up to the standards set by that design. Designated the Greater Underwater Propulsion Program (GUPPY), this included streamlining the hull and superstructure, removing unnecessary protuberances, increasing battery power, and fitting a schnorkel. In combination, these measures resulted in increased range and much better underwater speeds.

Initially, a number of boats of the Balao and Tench classes were modernized under the Guppy I programme; none of these now remains. In 1948-50, eight more Balao and Tench boats were converted direct to Guppy II standard, while five unfinished hulls were completed as new Guppy IIs. Finally, two Guppy Is were converted to Guppy II. Seven of the Guppy II remain: Argentina, one; Brazil, three; Taiwan, two; Venezuela, one.

Next in chronological order was the Guppy IA programme, in which ten more of the Balao and Tench classes were modernized. One of these (USS *Chopper*) achieved some fame by setting an involuntary

Above: Converted to Guppy standard, the Tench class USS *Pickerel* (SS-524) displays remarkable manoeuvrability by deliberately surfacing at a 48-degree up-angle from a depth of 150ft (46m) during tests on 1 March 1952.

Right: Balao class USS *Cubera* (SS-347), a Guppy II conversion, on a fleet exercise in 1961. Transferred to Venezuela in January 1972, she has now been stricken, but Venezuela retains one Guppy II: ex USS *Grenadier* (SS-525), refitted in Argentina, 1979-1980.

record on 11 February 1969, when it went into a sharp-angle descent to a depth of about 1,000ft (305m) before it could be brought back to the surface. This exceeded its design maximum depth of 412ft (126m) by a very considerable margin. Four of these boats remain in service: Argentina, one; Peru, two; Turkey, one.

In 1952-54, the Guppy IIA programme involved the conversion of a further sixteen of the Balao and Tench classes. This is now the largest remaining group, with eleven still in service: Greece, one; Spain, three; Turkey, seven.

Finally, nine Guppy II boats were further converted to Guppy III standard in 1960-62; ie, two to four years after the launching of the Barbel class. Plans for the conversion of more old submarines were dropped when the decision was made in favour of an all nuclear-powered submarine force. Six Guppy IIIs remain: Brazil, two; Greece, one; Italy, one; Turkey, two.

Most of these submarines can be expected to reach the end of their useful lives in the near future, and there is much competition among submarine exporting countries for this potentially lucrative market.

Abtao Class

Total built:	Four.
Launched:	1953-57.
Status:	Four in service (Peru).
Displacement:	825 tons (surfaced); 1,400 tons (submerged).
Dimensions:	Length, 243ft (74.1m); beam, 22ft (6.7m); draught, 14ft (4.3m).
Torpedo tubes:	Six 21in (533mm) (4 bow, 2 stern).
Gun:	One 5in (127mm) (*Abtao* and *Dos de Mayo*).
Propulsion:	Diesel, two (2,400bhp); electric, two.
Shafts:	Two.
Speed:	16kt, 30km/hr (surfaced); 10kt, 18.5km/hr (submerged).
Complement:	40.

In the early 1950s the US Navy built two small submarines of the Mackerel class for anti-submarine warfare training. These were 131ft 2in (40m) long with a submerged displacement of 347 tons and were the smallest submarines built for the US Navy since 1909. It is not clear why, when the Peruvian Navy sought new submarines in 1951, instead of ordering some of the many World War II boats available 'off-the-shelf' and at bargain prices, it decided instead to buy a stretched version of the Mackerel class, which was built for Peru by the Electric Boat Company as the Abtao class.

Two of the boats were refitted in 1965 and the others in 1968. Despite this they still have a submerged speed of only 10 knots, totally inadequate for today's needs, even in South American waters. As a unique eccentricity, two of the class mount a 5in (127mm) gun abaft the fin; so far as can be ascertained, they are the last submarines in the world to do so. They will doubtless be replaced by new West German-built Type 1200 submarines at an early date.

Below: US-built Peruvian patrol boat *Iquique*, Abtao class.

Bottom: Note *Abtao's* unique feature: a 5in (127mm) gun aft.

Tang Class/Darter Class/ Grayback Class/Barbel Class

Total built: Tang: 6; Darter: 1; Grayback: 2; Barbel: 3.
Launched: Tang: 1951-52; Darter: 1956; Grayback: 1957;
Barbel: 1958-59.
Status: Tang: 4 in service, 2 in reserve;
Darter: 1 in service; Grayback: 1 in service;
Barbel: 3 in service.
Displacement: Tang: 2,050 tons (surfaced); 2,700 tons
(submerged).
Darter: 1,720 tons (surfaced); 2,388 tons
(submerged).
Grayback: 2,670 tons (surfaced); 3,650 tons
(submerged).
Barbel: 2,145 tons (surfaced); 2,894 tons
(submerged).
Dimensions: Tang: length, 287ft (87.5m); beam, 27ft 4in
(8.3m); draught, 19ft (5.8m).
Darter: length, 284ft 6in (86.7m); beam, 27ft 2in
(8.3m); draught, 19ft (5.8m).
Grayback: length, 334ft (101.8m); beam, 27ft 2in
(8.3m); draught, 19ft (5.8m).
Barbel: length, 219ft 1in (66.8m); beam, 29ft
(8.8m); draught, 28ft (8.5m).
Torpedo tubes: Tang/Darter/Grayback: eight 21in (533mm);
Barbel: six 21in (533mm).
Propulsion: Tang: diesel, three (4,500bhp); electric, two
(5,600shp).
Darter/Grayback: diesel, three (4,500bhp);
electric, two (5,500shp).
Barbel: diesel, three (4,800bhp); electric, two
(3,150 shp).
Shafts: Tang/Darter/Grayback: two; Barbel: one.
Speed: Tang: 15.5kt, 28.5km/hr (surfaced); 16kt,
29.5km/hr (submerged).
Darter: 19.5kt, 36km/hr (surfaced); 14kt,
26km/hr (submerged).
Grayback: 20kt, 37km/hr (surfaced); 16.7kt,
31km/hr (submerged).
Barbel: 15kt, 28km/hr (surfaced); 21kt, 39km/hr
(submerged).
Complement: Tang: 83; Darter: 83; Grayback: 89; Barbel: 77.

Below: USS *Tang* (SS-563), now in reserve, seen here in 1959.

Only six conventional submarines now remain in the active inventory of the US Navy: three Barbel class, one Darter, one Grayback and one Tang. With the last conventional boat having been launched in 1959 (USS *Blueback* of the Barbel class), it now seems unlikely that any more will be built, except perhaps for research.

The Tang class of six boats was built in the early 1950s and, like the Soviet Whiskeys and French Narvals, it was closely based on the German Type XXI. Following many years of service with the US Navy, including several refits and modernizations, most of the Tangs are still active. Two are serving with the Italian Navy, but are due to be deleted in 1983-84. One was lent to Turkey for five years in 1980. The fourth (USS *Gudgeon*) remains in service with the US Navy as an SSAG. The remaining two are in reserve following the cancellation of a proposed sale to Iran.

The Darter class was to have comprised three boats, but in the event only one (USS *Darter*) was completed as a patrol submarine. Very similar in design to the Tang class, her lines show an equal debt to the German Type XXI submarine. *Darter* is due to be transferred to the reserve fleet in 1982.

The two boats of the Grayback class were modified from the Darter class while building and were completed as SSGs to launch Regulus missiles. Only USS *Grayback* remains. She was converted to a transport submarine, with a special compartment to carry seven officers and 60 soldiers, in 1967. Although reclassified in 1975 as an attack submarine (SS), she retains the troop compartment and is 'home-ported' at Subic Bay in the Philippines. She obviously has the potential to take part in clandestine operations, and, so far as is known, is the only submarine of her kind.

The Barbel class will almost certainly go down in history as the last conventional submarines to be built for the US Navy. They have the 'tear-drop' hull tested by USS *Albacore,* which gives high underwater speed for a non-nuclear submarine. The Tang class described above, built between 1949-52 and based on the Type XXI, have a submerged speed of 16-18 knots: the Barbels can better this by some 5-6 knots, although at the expense of performance on the surface. The Barbels still perform a useful function for the US Navy, acting as training boats, demonstrating the problems and abilities of conventional submarines in exercises with the rest of the fleet. The general Barbel design has been followed abroad in several classes; eg, the Japanese Uzushio and the Dutch Zwaardvis.

Above: Like many other boats designed in the late 1940s, the USN's Tang class was closely based on the German Type XXI.

Below left: As seen here, USS *Grayback* was completed in 1958 as an SSG to carry and launch the Regulus cruise missile.

Below: USS *Barbel* (SS-580) at speed; the distinctive 'teardrop' hull form is evident in this photograph.

Sutjeska Class/Heroj Class/ Sava Class

Total built: Sutjeska: 2; Heroj: 3; Sava: 2.
Launched: Sutjeska: 1958-59; Heroj: 1967-69; Sava: 1977.
Status: Sutjeska: 2 in service; Heroj: 3 in service; Sava: 2 in service.
Displacement: Sutjeska: 820 tons (surfaced), 945 tons (submerged).
Heroj: 1,068 tons (submerged).
Sava: 964 tons (submerged).
Dimensions: Sutjeska: length, 196ft 10in (60m); beam, 22ft 4in (6.8m); draught, 16ft 1in (4.9m).
Heroj: length, 210ft (64m); beam, 23ft 7in (7.2m); draught, 16ft 5in (5m).
Sava: length, 215ft 10in (65.8m); beam, 22ft 11in (7m); draught, 18ft (5.5m).
Torpedo tubes: Sutjeska/Heroj/Sava: six 21in (533mm).
Propulsion: Sutjeska: diesel (1,800hp), electric;
Heroj: diesel (2,400hp), electric;
Sava: diesel, electric.
Shafts: Sutjeska: two; Heroj/Sava: one.
Speed: Sutjeska: 14kt, 26km/hr (surfaced); 9kt, 16.5km/hr (submerged).
Heroj: 16kt, 29.5km/hr (surfaced); 10kt, 18.5km/hr (submerged).
Sava: not known (surfaced); 16kt, 29.5km/hr (submerged).
Complement: Sutjeska: 38; Heroj: 55; Sava: 35.

The Yugoslavs tend to keep a low profile where weapons manufacture is concerned, but it is known that they have some very competent designers and good production facilities in many fields. For many years following World War II, the only submarine of note in the Yugoslav fleet was the *Sava*, an ex-Italian boat which had been sunk in 1944, recovered by the Yugoslav Navy and rebuilt with a new conning-tower. She was scrapped in the 1970s.

Based on experience with *Sava*, the Uljanick yard at Pula designed and built the first-ever Yugoslav submarines: *Sutjeska* and *Neretva*. These are conventional boats, designed for use in the Mediterranean and Adriatic, their most unusual feature being a sharply slanting front to the conning-tower. During modernization in the late 1960s they were fitted with Soviet weapons systems and electronics.

Some ten years after the Sutjeska class came the three boats of the Heroj class, with a much cleaner hull and a streamlined fin. The published submerged speed of 10 knots seems rather low. As with the modernized Sutjeska class, much Soviet ancillary equipment is fitted.

The latest products of the Shipyard and Diesel Factory (S and DE) at Split are the two boats of the Sava class, of which the name-boat was commissioned in 1978. They are capable of diving to 1,000ft (305m) and have a submerged speed of 16 knots. Yugoslavia is prepared to export defence equipment, and the Sava class could well attract navies looking for a new conventional submarine from a source other than a major power. Unfortunately, however, these submarines are extensively equipped with Soviet electronics and weapons and there have been widely-publicized problems over spares for such equipment in the past.

Below left: Heroj class patrol submarine *Junak*, launched 1968.
Below: Sutjeska class *Neretva;* note sharply slanted fin.

Bottom: *Sava*, name-boat of Yugoslavia's latest patrol class.

OTHER SUPER-VALUE GUIDES IN THIS SERIES......

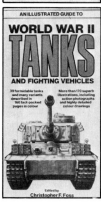

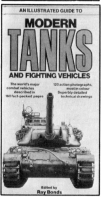

OTHER ILLUSTRATED MILITARY GUIDES NOW AVAILABLE....

Allied Fighters of World War II
Axis Fighters of World War II
Bombers of World War II
Modern Fighters
Modern Soviet Air Force
Modern US Air Force
Modern Warships
Soviet Ground Forces

✳ Each has 160 fact-filled pages
✳ Each is colourfully illustrated with hundreds of action photographs and technical drawings
✳ Each contains concisely presented data and accurate descriptions of major international weapons
✳ Each represents tremendous value

Further titles in this series are in preparation
Your military library will be incomplete without them.

PRINTED IN BELGIUM BY

INTERNATIONAL BOOK PRODUCTION